# 14
# PROVEN
# STEPS TO
# BUSINESS
# SUCCESS

## BY CLAY CLARK

RUSH TO
REVENUE
Money Cures
All Problems

BOOM: 14 Proven Steps to Business Success
ISBN 978-1-7342296-8-4
Copyright © 2021 by Clay Clark

Thrive Publishing

Published by Thrive Publishing
1100 Suite #100 Riverwalk Terrace
Jenks, OK 74037

Thrive Publishing books may be purchased for educational, business or sales promotional use. For more information, please email the Special Markets Department at info@ThriveTimeShow.com. For a good time visit ThriveTimeShow.com

"Today is the day you will learn how to turn your American Dream into a reality. Much like you, most people have a big vision but they don't know how to break their dream into the small action steps needed to turn their dream into a reality. Today is the day you begin learning the small and practical action steps needed to achieve success."

-Clay Clark

# How a Business Works

**F6 GOALS**
1. Faith
2. Family
3. Friendship
4. Fitness
5. Finances
6. Fun

"Rush to Revenue"
Money Cures All Problems

# The Road Map

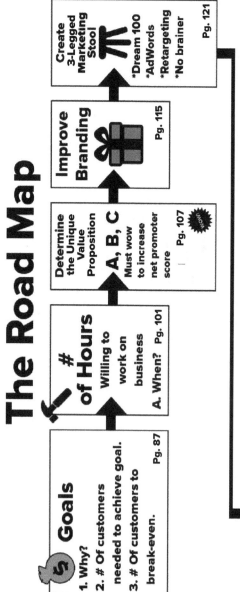

**Goals**
1. Why?
2. # Of customers needed to achieve goal.
3. # Of customers to break-even.
Pg. 87

**# of Hours**
Willing to work on business
A. When? Pg. 101

**Determine the Unique Value Proposition**
A, B, C
Must wow to increase net promoter score
Pg. 107

**Improve Branding**
Pg. 115

**Create 3-Legged Marketing Stool**
*Dream 100
*AdWords
*Retargeting
*No brainer
Pg. 121

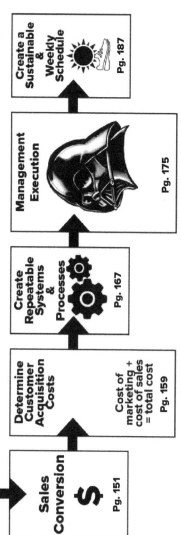

**Sales Conversion**
$
Pg. 151

**Determine Customer Acquisition Costs**
Cost of marketing + cost of sales = total cost
Pg. 159

**Create Repeatable Systems & Processes**
Pg. 167

**Management Execution**
Pg. 175

**Create a Sustainable & Weekly Schedule**
Pg. 187

# CONTENTS

**Welcome to the start of your success story.** Discipline is the bridge between dreams and accomplishment. Remember it's hard to build a reputation based on what you intend to do. Let's go dominate and get stuff done.

**Clay Clark**

**I'm Thom Clark's son. I miss you Dad.**

My father died after a long battle with ALS in 2016.

"Rush to Revenue"
Money Cures
All Problems

# WHO IS CLAY CLARK?

Clay is the former U.S. SBA Entrepreneur of the Year, Co-Host of the ThriveTimeShow.com Radio Show, and the founder of ThriveTimeShow.com. Over the course of his career, he has been a founding team member of many successful companies including DJConnection. com, EITRLounge.com, MakeYourLifeEpic.com, ThriveTimeShow.com, and EpicPhotos.com (Dallas, Oklahoma City, etc.). He and his companies have been featured in Forbes, Fast Company, Entrepreneur, PandoDaily, Bloomberg TV, Bloomberg Radio, the Entrepreneur On Fire Podcast, the So Money Podcast with Farnoosh Torabi, and on countless media outlets. He's been the speaker of choice for Hewlett-Packard, Maytag University, O'Reilly Auto Parts, Valspar Paint, Farmers Insurance, and many other companies. He is the father of five kids and he is the proud owner of 40 chickens, six ducks, four cats, and Thousands of trees. Clay is an obsessive New England Patriots fan and Tim Tebow apologist. He wears a basketball jersey every day. When not chasing his kids and wife around, he enjoys reading business case studies and autobiographies about successful entrepreneurs while burning pinion wood.

**U.S. Small Business Administration**

## SBA

*Your Small Business Resource*

### Oklahoma District Office

301 NW 6ᵗʰ Street, Suite 116  Oklahoma City, OK  73102   405/609-8000   (fax) 405/609-8990

---

February 21, 2007

Mr. Clayton Thomas Clark
DJ Connection Tulsa, Inc.
8900 South Lynn Lane Road
Broken Arrow, Oklahoma 74102

Dear Mr. Clark:

Congratulations!  You have been selected as the **2007 Oklahoma SBA Young Entrepreneur of the Year**.  On behalf of the U.S. Small Business Administration (SBA), I wish to express our appreciation for your support of small business and for your contributions to the economy of this State.

In recognition of your achievement, **an awards luncheon will be held Tuesday, May 22, 2007** at Rose State College in Midwest City, Okla. The luncheon is sponsored by the Oklahoma Small Business Development Center. Two complimentary luncheon tickets have been reserved for you and one guest.

Arrangements for the luncheon are still being finalized.  You will be notified of the details as soon as they become available.  You are encouraged to bring family, friends, and business associates.  Upon presentation of your award, you will have the opportunity to make acceptance comments.

Also, for our awards brochure, please email an electronic photo of yourself to darla.booker@sba.gov by Friday, March 16.

Again, congratulations on your outstanding accomplishment.

Sincerely,

*Dottie Overal*

Dorothy (Dottie) A. Overal
Oklahoma District Director

---

> Success is a choice. A choice to make trade-offs... a choice to get up early... a choice to skip lunch to hit a deadline... a choice to push through fear... a choice to work on the weekend to get ahead... a choice to turn off the TV and open a book... a choice to hold yourself and others accountable... success is a choice that I make every day.

**CLAY CLARK**
*Founder of ThriveTimeShow.com, former U.S. SBA Entrepreneur of the Year, host of the ThriveTime Show, and America's #1 Business Coach*

# The F6 Life
## DESIGN THE LIFE YOU WANT OR LIVE THE LIFE YOU DON'T WANT BY DEFAULT.

Psalm 118:24

"This is the day that the Lord has made. We will rejoice and be glad in it."

# F6

### What are Your F6 Goals?

The Bonus Secret F

Fun Goals — When?_____

Finance Goals — When?_____

Fitness Goals — When?_____

Friendship Goals — When?_____

Family Goals — When?_____

Faith Goals — When?_____

"Control your destiny or someone else will."

**JACK WELCH**
*Former CEO of GE who grew the company by 4,000% during his tenure as CEW*

## What is your biggest limiting factor?

## What questions do you have?

Be a Business Duck!

# THE EMOTIONAL
## TRADEOFFS OF A SUCCESSFUL PERSON

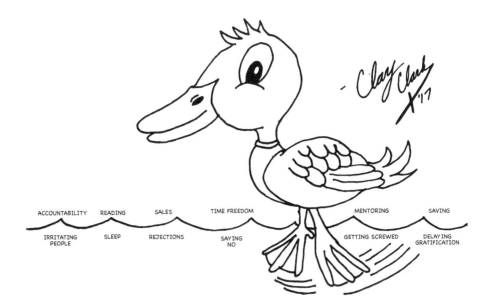

| ACCOUNTABILITY | READING | SALES | TIME FREEDOM | MENTORING | SAVING |
|---|---|---|---|---|---|
| IRRITATING PEOPLE | SLEEP | REJECTIONS | SAYING NO | GETTING SCREWED | DELAYING GRATIFICATION |

# NOTES

_____
_____
_____
_____
_____
_____
_____
_____
_____
_____
_____
_____
_____
_____
_____
_____
_____
_____
_____
_____
_____
_____

# BE COACHABLE

## WE KNOW THE PROVEN PATH

**WE KNOW THE PROVEN PATH ALPHABETICALLY SPEAKING**

AZ Medical
BankRegent.com
Drzoellner.com
DJConnection.com
EITRLounge
MakeYourLifeEpic.com

"Nothing is as powerful as a changed mind."

**TD JAKES**
*Bestselling author and pastor of the Potter's House.*

Storytime:

The Stress of life before GPS and the consequences
of not knowing where you are going

RUSH TO REVENUE
*Money Cures All Problems*

# What is your biggest limiting factor?

"One of the main reasons people don't improve is that they are not honest with themselves."

**LEE COCKERELL**

*Thrive15.com mentor and investor and the former Executive Vice President of Operations for the Walt Disney World Resort. As the Senior Operating Executive for ten years Lee led a team of 40,000 Cast Members and was responsible for the operations of 20 resort hotels, 4 theme parks, 2 water parks, a shopping and entertainment village and the ESPN sports and recreation complex.*

Having personally grown dozens of successful businesses, I know the importance of being coachable. Having been invited to speak or consult with America's largest and most successful companies including Maytag University, O'Reilly's Auto Parts, Hewlett Packard, Valspar Paint, Chevron, UPS, etc…I have witnessed firsthand how thirsty for knowledge and coachable the top business leaders are. Having personally spoken to and coached hundreds of clients and thousands of workshop / conference attendees on how to grow a successful business **I NEED TO CHALLENGE YOU HERE TO BECOME COACHABLE.**

**I NEED TO CHALLENGE YOU HERE.** I NEED TO CHALLENGE YOU TO COMMIT TO NOT LETTING YOUR OWN EMOTIONS, THE EMOTIONS OF OTHERS, AND EXCUSES YOU MAKE FOR YOURSELF TO CAUSE YOU TO DANGEROUSLY DRIFT AND TO NEGATIVELY TRANSFORM YOU INTO BECOMING BOTH UNCOACHABLE AND PIG-HEADED IN YOUR WRONGNESS THAT HAS RESULTED IN YOU CONSISTENTLY BEING UNABLE TO PRODUCE THE RESULTS THAT YOU SEEK. If you do a quick Google search, you will quickly discover that Forbes reports eight out of ten businesses fail. From my first-hand experience, I believe that 8 out of 10 business owners fail because they are uncoachable. However, I can empathize with what it is like to be uncoachable because I was once uncoachable too. And I suffered because of it.

> "Most real failures are due to limitations which men set up in their own minds."

**NAPOLEON HILL**
*The author of the number one best-selling self-help author of all time, Think and Grow Rich, and the man whom my son is named after Aubrey Napoleon-Hill Clark*

Before I had mentors like David Robinson, Doctor Zoellner, Lee Cockerell, and Clifton Taulbert in my life, I was a "happy hoper" and not a "diligent doer." I once falsely believed that my own lack of success was the result of losing the genetic lottery. I used to believe I could not raise the capital I needed to grow my business because of my lack of luck and the fact that I grew up without money. I used to believe that my lack of sales results were based upon my unchangeable "God-given personality." While building my first business, I used to lazily believe that my lack of leads were the result of not "having enough word of mouth" which is impossible to generate if you don't have any customers yet.

> "Ninety-nine percent of the failures come from people who have the habit of making excuses."

**GEORGE WASHINGTON CARVER**
*A famous American botanist and inventor whose birthday was unknown because he was born into slavery in Missouri. What excuses could he have made for himself?*

> "To me job titles don't matter. Everyone is in sales. It's the only way we stay in business."

**HARVEY MACKEY**
*Best selling author and award winning entrepreneur*

I used to falsely and ignorantly (I did not know better) believe that my website's rank in Google was one of those things I could not control. I used to believe that my chronic lateness was due to the weather, the traffic, or something I ate the night before. I used to believe my lack of success was all justifiable and not something that I could ever control. Because most people are not successful, they patted me on the back and said the following poverty creating and justifying statements to me:

## POVERTY CREATING MINDSETS AND JUSTIFICATION STATEMENTS:

1. "You don't need to give that speech. I know you've always struggled with stammering and stuttering."

2. "Hey you overslept don't worry about it. Maybe you are just not a morning person."

3. "Well, maybe it's just not meant to be."

4. "It takes money to make money."

5. "Stop striving so hard and focus on what really matters."

6. "Your sales are down because the company's culture isn't right... it's just too hard to manage millennials..."

7. "Maybe managing people, dealing with confrontation, and managing the numbers is just not your thing."

8. "Don't feel bad. You probably just don't have time to read all of that stuff right now...you have so much going on in your life with the upcoming wedding and all..."

9. "Don't sweat it...I know I couldn't focus on running a business if my best friend friend was suddenly killed in a car accident either."

10. "Hey, maybe you shouldn't do a radio show this year. I know that I personally couldn't focus on writing outlines if I knew my Dad was dying from ALS (Lou Gehrig's Disease) either.

11. "Once you hit your financial goals, you need to sit down and really plan out what you want to do with the rest of your life."

12. "It's too late for you to do that with your career. You need to be realistic."

13. "You really can't go around saying that stuff or you are going to irritate half of your potential customers."

And then, when I finally was able to get in-person coaching from millionaires, mentors, and real-life entrepreneurs who had been able to turn their dreams into reality, I was told uncomfortable wealth-creating and excuse-destroying statements like:

## $ WEALTH CREATING MINDSETS AND PERSONAL $ ACCOUNTABILITY STATEMENTS:

1. "You can either get bitter or better. The choice is yours."
   **Clifton Taulbert** (*An African American man who was not allowed to go into banks as a kid due to legal segregation and who went on to start his own bank*)

2. "With self-discipline almost anything can be achieved in every aspect of life."
   **Lee Cockerell** (*Thrive15.com investor, author, and the former Executive Vice President of Walt Disney World Resorts who never fails to deliver tough love when needed*)

3. "When you do hard things life gets easier."
   **Lee Cockerell** (*A man who diligently worked his way up from the bottom of the Marriott Hotels payroll to being the head of Walt Disney World Resorts and being responsible for managing 40,000 team members*)

4. "If you can't delay gratification, save money, and build your war chest, then you will lose."

   **Doctor Robert Zoellner** (*The man who started out washing dishes at a Mexican restaurant and who has now built the region's most successful auto auction, optometry clinic, horse-breeding facility, and numerous other successful small businesses*)

5. "You either pay now or pay later with just about every decision you make about where and how you spend your time."

   **Lee Cockerell** (*Thrive15.com investor and the man who once drove to a speaking event while wearing a colostomy bag after surgery so that he wouldn't miss his speaking event*)

6. "Whatever you accept is what you should expect."

   **Doctor Robert Zoellner** (*The closest thing I have to a living father, the Thrive15. com CEO, and the optometrist-turned Tulsa business tycoon who now co-hosts the ThriveTime Show with me every day for two hours of power. You can listen to all of the archived podcasts at ThriveTimeShow.com*)

7. "One way to get your priorities accomplished is to schedule them into your calendar."
   **Lee Cockerell** (*The former Executive Vice President of Walt Disney World Resorts*)

8. "Rich people have big libraries, poor people have big TVs."

   **Doctor Robert Zoellner** (*The Thrive15.com CEO, and the optometrist-turned Tulsa business tycoon who now co-hosts the ThriveTime Show with me every day for two hours of power. You can listen to all of the archived podcasts at ThriveTimeShow.com*)

9. "I know this is tough buddy, but you have to stay focused and deliver. Your Dad is going to die a slow and painful death unless God works a miracle. Call me and we'll MAN-CAVE it this weekend."

   **Doctor Robert Zoellner** (*My business partner and the man who is the closest thing I have to a living father*)

10. "Your customers hold you to a high standard. If you want to achieve true excellence, raise that bar even higher for yourself, your colleagues, and everyone around you."
**Lee Cockerell** (*The former Executive Vice President of Walt Disney World Resorts who once was responsible for managing over 40,000 humans. Could you even imagine that?*)

11. "Your happiness comes from designing and living the life you want right now. When are you going to lose that suit?"
**Doctor Robert Zoellner** (*A man who began wearing soccer jerseys and casual clothes every day as soon he was able to build a business system that was capable of producing revenue for him when he was not personally seeing patients*)

12. "The quality of your life is directly affected by how and where you spend your time."
**Lee Cockerell** (*The former Executive Vice President of Walt Disney World Resorts who once built the systems needed to help him manage Walt Disney World Resorts and the nearly one million customers (guests) that visit their theme parks each week*)

13. "You need to focus on providing business school without the bs to entrepreneurs and wantrepreneurs in a real, raw, and unfiltered way like you always have."
**Doctor Robert Zoellner** (*A man who routinely uses that side of his massive optometry clinic located next to Oklahoma's most bustling mall to promote his political candidate of choice without worrying about the 50% of people that his pro-capitalist candidates may often upset*)

# Everybody Needs a Coach

"The advice that sticks out I got from John Doerr, who in 2001 said, "My advice to you is to have a coach." The coach he said I should have is Bill Campbell. I initially resented the advice, because after all, I was a CEO. I was pretty experienced. Why would I need a coach? Am I doing something wrong? My argument was, How could a coach advise me if I'm the best person in the world at this? But that's not what a coach does. The coach doesn't have to play the sport as well as you do. They have to watch you and get you to be your best. In the business context a coach is not a repetitious coach. A coach is somebody who looks at something with another set of eyes, describes it to you in [his] words, and discusses how to approach the problem."

**ERIC SCHMIDT**
*The CEO and Chairman of Google in FORTUNE Magazine*

## THE GROWTH-FOCUSED MINDSET OF A SUCCESSFUL ENTREPRENEUR

Every day you invest 1 to 2 hours planning out your day, organizing your life, and self-examining where you are and where you want to be in the areas of Faith, Family, Friendships, Fitness, Fun, and Finances. YOU ARE COACHABLE when it comes to learning and executing the proven routines, strategies, systems, and habits of successful people. You are intentional every day about designing and living the life you want to live. You feel in control of where you are going because although life may have given you difficult circumstances you know that you are in control of how you choose to respond to them. You understand and embrace that strength comes as a result of struggle. You understand and embrace the exponentially compounding power of scheduling daily diligence into your life. You know how to consistently apply effort even on the days when you don't feel like it. You recognize that it is up to you to seek out wise counsel from mentors who know the proven path to speed up the achievement of your success and to avoid running over the landmines that have already been well-marked by those who have gone before you. You are on time all the time and typically 15 minutes early. You rule your emotions and are not ruled by them. YOU, MY FRIEND, ARE COACHABLE.

"A Carnegie or a Rockefeller or a James J. Hill or a Marshall Field accumulates a fortune through the application of the same principles available to all of us, but we envy them and their wealth without ever thinking of studying their philosophy and applying it to ourselves. We look at a successful person in the hour of their triumph and wonder how they did it, but we overlook the importance of analyzing their methods and we forget the price they had to pay in the careful and well-organized preparation that had to be made before they could reap the fruits of their efforts."

**NAPOLEON HILL**
*The best-selling author of Think & Grow Rich, the personal apprentice of Andrew Carnegie, and the personal mentor of Oral Roberts*

RUSH TO REVENUE
Money Cures All Problems

# Dysfunctional Mindsets

**PREDICTABLE, PROBLEMATIC, AND CORRECTABLE PEOPLE PATTERNS OF THE UNCOACHABLE ENTREPRENEUR:**

> Circle which dysfunctional mindset best describes your former self or YOU if you are not intentional about being personally coachable and accountable.

## DYSFUNCTIONAL MINDSET #1
## THE EMPLOYEE-MINDSET ENTREPRENEUR

You want to be a successful entrepreneur, but you desperately want to be told that you can keep the same schedule that you had when you were a 9 to 5 employee because "you value life balance." Just like when you worked for someone else, anytime that there is snow on the road, you want to "call in and request off for safety reasons" for your own business. You want to take the day off before every major holiday and the day after every after major holiday and you are even tempted to take off those quasi-holidays that all B-level employees like (Columbus Day, etc.).

You desperately want the law of sowing and reaping not to apply during the massive amounts of days that you take off and you want to be told that once you learn the "success secrets" you are going to have a hall pass through life and that the law of cause and effect will no longer impact the results that you see in your life. My friend, this can absolutely be the year that you will achieve the success that you desire, however, you must be willing to make changes.

According to an article published by Business Insider called, *Check Out How Much the Average American Works Each Year Compared to the French, the Germans and The Koreans* the average American is now working approximately 1,680 hours per year, which if you are dividing that by 40 hours per week means that the average American only works 42 weeks per year.

RUSH TO REVENUE
Money Cures All Problems

If you take off for your birthday, your spouse's birthday, your anniversary, the days before and after each national holiday, two weeks for vacation, and when you don't feel good while starting or growing a business (before you make your millions), you will be poor.

## Circle the days you took off this past year from sowing seeds, and determine how realistic it is for you to plan on reaping a harvest this year.

The day before New Year's Eve.

New Year's Eve.

New Year's Day.

The day after New Year's Day.

The day before Martin Luther King, Jr. Day

Martin Luther King, Jr. Day

The day after Martin Luther King, Jr. Day

The day before President's Day

President's Day

The day after President's Day

The Thursday before Good Friday

Good Friday

The Saturday before Easter

Easter

The day after Easter

The day before Memorial Day

Memorial Day

The day after Memorial Day

The day before Independence Day

Independence Day

The day after Independence Day

The day before Labor Day

Labor Day

The day after Labor Day

The day before Columbus Day

Columbus Day

The day after Columbus Day

The day before Veterans' Day

Veterans' Day

The day after Veterans' Day

The Monday of the week of Thanksgiving

The Tuesday of the week of Thanksgiving

The Wednesday of the week of Thanksgiving

Thanksgiving

Black Friday

The day before Christmas Eve (Known as Festivus for all of your Seinfeld fans)

Christmas Eve

Christmas Day

The day after Christmas

7 days that you don't feel like coming in because you feel sick

104 weekend days off

"You can't get much done in life if you only work on the days when you feel good."

**JERRY WEST**
*Hall of Fame basketball player and legendary NBA executive*

"Lazy hands make for poverty, but diligent hands bring wealth."

**PROVERBS 10:4**

"Rise and Grind."

**CLAY CLARK**

## DYSFUNCTIONAL MINDSET #2
## THE AGGRESSIVE, CRITICAL, AND DEMANDING
## OF IMMEDIATE IMPOSSIBLE RESULTS
## ENTREPRENEUR:

You don't like the concept that over a 25 year period of time, one man with diligence could build the state's most successful auto auction, the state's most profitable optometry clinic, one of the state's most successful horse-breeding facilities, a successful durable medical equipment company, a diagnostic sleep center, a booming online business school, and a syndicated radio show... and frankly it irritates you... because you want to build and experience the success of these businesses at once. After all, you see business opportunities everywhere. You've pounded the energy drinks, attended money-magnet seminars, watched the Tony Robbins and Tai Lopez videos and now you want to earn the money that you deserve immediately. You aren't fond of gravity, you believe that you deserve to be able to fly, and you just know that your business idea would go "viral" if you just had the funding.

**YOU WANT TO KNOW THE PROVEN PATH UP THE MOUNTAIN TO BUSINESS SUCCESS AND YOU WANT OTHER PEOPLE TO CARRY YOU UP THE MOUNTAIN AS WELL.** You want the reward, but you don't want the struggle.

"Most people are sitting on their own diamond mines. The surest ways to lose your diamond mine are to get bored, become overambitious, or start thinking that the grass is greener on the other side. Find your core focus, stick to it, and devote your time and resources to excelling at it."

**GINO WICKMAN**
*Best-selling author of Traction: Get a Grip on Your Business*

## DYSFUNCTIONAL MINDSET #3
## THE CHRONICALLY-DISTRACTED
## ENTREPRENEUR:

You want to focus and pay attention, but you just received a notification on your phone that you want to check real quick. You know that you, and you alone, must create the 1,000 words of content that Google needs you to have on every page of your website to enhance your search engine score, but you updated your Facebook status and got into a 45 minute conversation with one of your employees about how they feel instead. You've also recently discovered that it's also very hard to write while watching CNN's non-stop coverage of Hurricane "Who-Gives-A-Crap."

You were trying to read this section of the book, but somebody just liked your Facebook photo and you got distracted...

"We need to re-create boundaries. When you carry a digital gadget that creates a virtual link to the office, you need to create a virtual boundary that didn't exist before."

**DANIEL GOLEMAN**
*A world-renowned best-selling author, psychologist, and science journalist. For twelve years, he wrote for The New York Times, reporting on the brain and behavioral sciences. He is the author of the legendary book, Emotional Intelligence.*

## DYSFUNCTIONAL MINDSET #4
## KNOWLEDGEABLE, SKEPTICAL AND COMPLEX
## BUSINESSES WANT-TO-BE-LEADER:

You graduated from the University of Whatever with a BS (Bachelor of Science) Degree of Whatever, and you have come to the realization that the marketplace does not pay you based upon your academic resume. You know just enough about everything to wow your friends and to engage in an intelligent conversation with any random person that you've ever met on a plane. In the back of your mind, you are thinking... if this doesn't work out, I might need to go back to get my MBA.

You are in love with the vision and goal setting part of business (1% of the work), but you are not in love with the work ethic and process needed to produce the results you seek.

"You don't get paid for the hour. You get paid for the value you bring to the hour."

**JIM ROHN**
*Best-selling author and famous international speaker / sales trainer*

When I owned the nation's largest wedding entertainment and disc jockey company I did not know about speakers, or how they worked, but I did know how to build a successful business. Doctor Zoellner is not the world's best optometrist and does not actually see patients, yet his business sees more patients than any other optometry clinic in Tulsa. I have no interest in men's grooming, style or haircuts, yet I am a co-founder and CEO of one of the region's most successful chains of men's grooming and haircut lounges, The Elephant In The Room. Doctor Zoellner doesn't know how to maintain cars and does not have an automotive background, yet he owns one of the region's top auto auctions. How is it possible that his auction beats auto auctions owned by lifetime "car guys?" I built the nation's largest wedding photography company, yet I did not know what kind of cameras we used and how to even take photos up until the time I sold it. How is it possible that my photography business is exponentially more successful than the photography company's owned by photography gurus?

## DYSFUNCTIONAL MINDSET #5
## THE "NEVER ON-TIME" GUY:

Your life is just soooo busy that nobody could possibly understand how busy you are. Although I have five kids, 40 chickens, and 9 businesses I could never possibly understand how busy you are. Although my own father died of suffocation right in front of my eyes on September 5th, 2016 after a 1 year battle with ALS (Lou Gehrig's disease), I could not possibly understand how stressful your life is. Although my son was born blind, I could never understand how difficult your life is. And because of this, you seek validation and affirmation that somehow the law of sowing and reaping doesn't apply to you because of your "tough situation."

"It doesn't matter if you come from the inner city. People who fail in life are people who find lots of excuses. It's never too late for a person to recognize that they have potential in themselves."

**BEN CARSON**
*A legendary American surgeon whose life was turned into a movie*

"Lost time is never found again."

**BENJAMIN FRANKLIN**
*A man who accomplished much during his 84 years on the planet. Benjamin was an American polymath and one of the Founding Fathers of the United States. Franklin was a leading writer, printer, political philosopher, politician, Freemason, postmaster, scientist, inventor, humorist, civic activist, statesman, and diplomat*

RUSH TO REVENUE
Money Cures All Problems

## DYSFUNCTIONAL MINDSET #6
## THE "I'M NOT GOING TO DO MY ACTION ITEMS" GUY:

You believe that if you hop on a coaching call and learn the proven system without actually investing your personal time to apply anything that eventually things will just get done by themselves. You secretly believe that the science behind the Shake Weight and unicorns is plausible. You believe that your product is so good that it will sell itself and your company will magically build itself without involving you. You have subconsciously bought into the charlatan get-rich-quick-Tai-Lopez-earn-something-for-nothing-so-that-you-can-start-earning-$20,000-per-month-from-home-without-working philosophy of life which allows you to believe that it is possible to create copious amounts of sustainable wealth without investing the hours of hard work that are required to tediously build workflows, checklists, optimize your website, analyze your web traffic, hire people, fire people, do your accounting, and to receive the hundreds of rejections that you need to learn from enroute to actually selling your products at a profit to your ideal and likely buyers.

# The 80–100 Hour Work Week

"Lazy hands make for poverty, but diligent hands bring wealth."

**PROVERBS 10:4**

"All hard work brings a profit, but mere talk leads only to poverty."

**PROVERBS 14:23**

"Yet a little sleep, a little slumber, a little folding of the hands to sleep: So shall thy poverty come as one that travelleth, and thy want as an armed man. A naughty person, a wicked man, walketh with a froward mouth."

**PROVERBS 6:10-12**

## Charlatan

A person who falsely pretends to know or be something in order to deceive people.

"The three great essentials to achieve anything worthwhile are: Hard work, stick-to-itiveness, and common sense."

"Genius is one percent inspiration and ninety-nine percent perspiration."

**THOMAS EDISON**

*Many consider him to be the world's best inventor and half of you reading this consider him to be the man who stole Tesla's light bulb invention. He developed many devices that greatly influenced life around the world, including the phonograph, the motion picture camera, and the long-lasting, practical electric light bulb. Dubbed "The Wizard of Menlo Park."*

*Edison was one of the first inventors to apply the principles of mass production and large-scale teamwork to the process of invention, and because of that, he is often credited with the creation of the first industrial research laboratory. Edison held 1,093 US patents in his name, as well as patents all over the world. He founded General Electric and is responsible for essentially creating the industries involving: electric light, power utilities, recorded sound and the motion pictures (movies). It's arguable that without Edison, we would not have electric light, recorded sound, recorded motion pictures, or movies.*

RUSH TO
REVENUE
Money Cures
All Problems

## DYSFUNCTIONAL MINDSET #7
## THE "NON-EMOTIONALLY ENGAGED" GUY:

You don't want to admit that you are stuck and that you need help breaking through your biggest limiting factors, but you do recognize that you "may need some coaching" so you hesitantly have enrolled in a business coaching platform so that you can "try it out." You won't engage in the conversations with your coach or ever knock out your action items... because you are just seeing if this program can help you... This logic makes sense to you... I'm going to try out farming. I'm not going to do the hard work required to till the soil, to sow the seeds, or to water the seeds. I just want to see what this farming thing is all about and if the "tilling, sowing, watering, and reaping" theory actually works.

You want the financial freedom, the corner office, and time freedom that you will get as a result of producing a boatload of profits, but you are not willing to suffer through the sixty-hour workweeks filled with endless sales calls, staff recruitment, detailed paperwork, training, and workflow creation.

"Lazy hands make for poverty, but diligent hands bring wealth."

**PROVERBS 10:4**
*From that controversial book known as The Bible*

## DYSFUNCTIONAL MINDSET #8
## THE "I'M-GOING-TO-TRY-TO-SOLVE-ALL-OF-MY-BUSINESS-QUESTIONS-AT-ONCE" GUY:

You want to SOLVE ALL OF YOUR BUSINESS PROBLEMS NOW although every successful entrepreneur on the planet will tell you that you must simplify and focus on methodically knocking out the action items that will (move-the-needle) create the biggest impact in your business. For you, my friend, you must understand that the process of building a successful business is just that...a process.

"People think focus means saying yes to the thing you've got to focus on. But that's not what it means at all. It means saying no to the hundred other good ideas that there are. You have to pick carefully. I'm actually as proud of the things we haven't done as the things I have done. Innovation is saying no to 1,000 things."

**STEVE JOBS**
*Co-founder of Apple and the former CEO of PIXAR*

## DYSFUNCTIONAL MINDSET #9
## THE "EVERYTHING IS A BURNING FIRE" GUY:

You have never consistently blocked out the 1 to 2 hours per day that are REQUIRED to intentionally design a successful life one day and one action item at a time. You have not yet created the habit of diligently mapping out your day in a place and at a time where you will be un-interrupted by distractions. Thus, you are currently trying to do the impossible. You aren't blocking out the "quiet time," "planning time" or "meta-time" (the 2 hours of daily planning time) that every top entrepreneur needs for proactively planning out their day. Thus, the success that Lee Cockerell, Doctor Zoellner, and I have achieved is currently not possible for you. So...you secretly always feel like you are "running behind" and that everything is a burning fire. As your business grows, this will become an increasingly massive problem and will likely cause you to have a mental break-down at some point. I've seen this happen countless times. My friend, you must start proactively planning out and designing each successful day for your successful life. This "my-hair-is-on-fire" approach to life is going to keep you busy and furiously thrashing about without moving forward.

"One way to get your priorities accomplished is to schedule them into your calendar."

**LEE COCKERELL**
*The former Executive President of Walt Disney World Resorts that used to manage 40,000 cast members as the former Executive Vice President of Operations for Walt Disney World Resorts*

## DYSFUNCTIONAL MINDSET #10
## THE "CONSTANTLY-CALLING-TEXTING-AND-EMAILING- WITH-URGENT-ACTION-ITEMS" GUY:

You are new to business success and because 8 out of 10 businesses fail (according to Forbes), you've never personally witnessed the nitty gritty details of somebody actually starting and growing a successful business firsthand so this whole scheduled "meeting-once-a-week-thing" really frustrates you. You want to believe that Doctor Zoellner and I have created financial and time freedom by being accessible to each other and every member of our team 24-7. You want to believe that the REAL SECRET to our success has been just running from one burning fire to the next... and fortunately, that is not true. In fact, Doctor Zoellner and I don't email each other EVER unless it's to share a legal document. In fact, Doctor Zoellner and I don't text each other all day with show notes for our radio show, pictures of cats, or random burning fires. We have scheduled weekly times to meet with who we need to meet with. We have scheduled "rocks" into our schedule that must happen and we know the "Key Performance Indicators" that we must hold our teammates accountable to EVERYDAY.

"Successful businesses operate with a crystal clear vision that is shared by everyone. They have the right people in the right seats. They have a pulse on their operations by watching and managing a handful of numbers on a weekly basis. They identify and solve issues promptly in an open and honest environment. They document their processes and ensure that they are followed by everyone. They establish priorities for each employee and ensure that a high level of trust, communication, and accountability exists on each team."

**GINO WICKMAN**
*Best-selling author of Traction*

## DYSFUNCTIONAL MINDSET #11
## THE "MAD-AT-THE-MESSENGER" GUY:

The former communist leaders of the Soviet Union thought that the systematic redistribution of wealth through a government-mandated system was a great idea. They really didn't like it when they surveyed their people and found that most of their population was either unmotivated, literally starving, or passionately longing to go back to a time where the government didn't control everything. Thus, when their citizens told them negative feedback, they killed them. The people of planet Earth didn't like it when Jesus came to Earth and pointed out the truth, so they killed him. Racist people didn't like that Martin Luther King Jr. dared to say, "I have a dream that my four little children will one day live in a nation where they will not be judged by the color of their skin, but by the content of their character," so they assassinated him. So you now are tempted to do this same move, "attack-the-messenger."

With this mindset, when you hear uncomfortable truths about your business, you realize that this is the perfect time to attack the character or the resume of the coach presenting you with the simplicity and diligence required to implement the proven 13-point business system that both Doctor Zoellner and I have designed for ourselves and that we are now, for the first time, teaching to others like you.

"If you are going to tell people the truth, you had better be funny or it won't go over well."

**LEE COCKERELL**
*The former Executive Vice President of Walt Disney World Resorts who once successfully managed 40,000 employees and all of the personality types that comes with a large workforce*

## SUPER MOVES: HOW TO BE FUNNY

1. Shock and Awe / Physical Comedy
2. Self-Depreciation
3. Recovery
4. Jokes
5. Stories

# The Time Will Never be Just Right

"For all of the most important things, the timing always sucks. Waiting for a good time to quit your job? The stars will never align and the traffic lights of life will never all be green at the same time. The universe doesn't conspire against you, but it doesn't go out of its way to line up the pins either. Conditions are never perfect. "Someday" is a disease that will take your dreams to the grave with you. Pro and con lists are just as bad. If it's important to you and you want to do it "eventually," just do it and correct course along the way."

**TIM FERRISS**
*Best-selling author of the Four Hour Work Week, former venture capitalist, and one of the world's most successful podcasters*

## Put a check mark by the excuse that seems like the most viable reason that you cannot possibly become successful.

- [ ] Too Young
- [ ] Too Old
- [ ] No Connections
- [ ] No Capital
- [ ] No Time
- [ ] No Skills
- [ ] No ability to Focus
- [ ] Have to Wait Until Kids Go to School

- [ ] Don't Do Well with People
- [ ] Love People Too Much
- [ ] Afraid of Success
- [ ] Afraid of Failure
- [ ] Attention Deficit Disorder
- [ ] Obsessive Compulsive Disorder
- [ ] Too Chronically Fatigued

RUSH TO REVENUE
Money Cures All Problems

## DYSFUNCTIONAL MINDSET #12
## THE "I-CARE-ABOUT-WHAT-EVERYBODY-ELSE-THINKS-AND-SO-TO-AVOID-ANY-CONFRONTATION-EVER-I-NEVER-HOLD-PEOPLE-ACCOUNTABLE-NEVER-TAKE-A-STAND-FOR-ANYTHING-NEVER-FIRE-ANYBODY-AND-NEVER-CREATE-REMARKABLE-MARKETING-AND-COMPELLING-NO-BRAINER-OFFERS-NEEDED-TO-GET-YOUR-IDEAL-AND-LIKELY-BUYERS-TO-TAKE-THE-ACTION-YOU-WANT" GUY:

You've always been "a pleaser," and, generally, a well-liked person. Because you are not a psychopath, you actually have always cared about people, how you make people feel, and how people feel about you.

However, as an aspiring entrepreneur you have begun to realize that this "please everybody first" and "make sure everybody likes my idea before I do anything" mentality has consistently caused you to do nothing in an attempt to avoid criticism. If this is you, these are the repetitive problems that you find yourself dealing with every day:

### Psychopath
A person who is mentally ill, who does not care about other people, and who is usually dangerous or violent.

1. You struggle deciding on the market niche that you will focus on and cater to because you worry about excluding people that may get offended.

2. You struggle to launch aggressive marketing.

 "Being responsible sometimes means pissing people off."

**COLIN POWELL**

"In a crowded marketplace, fitting in is failing. In a busy marketplace, not standing out is the same as being invisible...If you're remarkable, then it's likely that some people won't like you. That's part of the definition of remarkable. Nobody gets unanimous praise -- ever. The best the timid can hope for is to be unnoticed. Criticism comes to those who stand out. Playing it safe. Following the rules. They seem like the best ways to avoid failure. Alas, that pattern is awfully dangerous. The current marketing "rules" will ultimately lead to failure."

**SETH GODIN**
*Best-selling author and marketing guru who sold his business Yoyodyne to Yahoo! For $30 million*

Ample Examples of Purple Cows:

The pricing of Starbucks coffee.

- Iced Coffee (with or without Milk) – Tall – $2.25
- Iced Coffee (with or without Milk) – Grande – $2.65
- Iced Coffee (with or without Milk) – Venti – $2.95
- Iced Coffee (with or without Milk) – Trenta – $3.45

The pricing of Apple products.

The jokes, pricing and advertising strategies of Southwest Airlines (do a Google search for "Southwest airlines flight attendant rap" and you will see what I'm talking about)

The volume, loudness and all-around testosterone of the Harley Davidson motorcycles.

The refusal of In-n-Out Burger to add chicken and ANY other items to their menu and their refusal to stop printing the Bible verses on their packaging (Proverbs 3:5, John 3:16, Revelation 3:20 and Nahum 1:7)

- "Trust in the LORD with all your heart and lean not on your own understanding." – Proverbs 3:5

- "For God so loved the world that he gave his one and only Son, that whoever believes in him shall not perish but have eternal life." – John 3:16

- "Here I am! I stand at the door and knock. If anyone hears my voice and opens the door, I will come in and eat with that person, and they with me." – Revelation 3:20

- "The Lord is good, a refuge in times of trouble. He cares for those who trust in him." – Nahum 1:7

The pricing of Champagne Armand de Brignac – $299 per bottle

The Marriott Hotel's insistence on putting The Bible and the Book of Mormon in every hotel room.

because you worry that it may upset your competition or somebody else inhabiting the planet Earth. In your mind, you often say, "I don't know if I should say that in my CALL TO ACTION OR HEADLINE because technically our service or product actually includes A, B, C and D, not just A, B and C…"

"Don't be distracted by criticism. Remember, the only taste of success some people have is when they take a bite out of you."

**ZIG ZIGLAR**
*Best-selling author, motivational speaker, and legendary sales trainer*

**3.** You struggle choosing the overhead music that is played in your office because Kevin keeps saying, "It's like we've heard the same songs every day. CAN WE PLEASE CHANGE THE MUSIC!"

"Great spirits have always encountered violent opposition from mediocre minds."

**ALBERT EINSTEIN**
*A German-born theoretical physicist. He developed the general theory of relativity, one of the two pillars of modern physics (alongside quantum mechanics)*

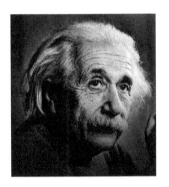

**4.** You struggle to get your staff to follow any expectations that you have for them. Your team members run around doing whatever they want regardless of what is outlined in your handbook. They don't follow your dress code, any processes, or any systems that you have ever created and thus, you always find yourself doing everything yourself because "they may not like being told what to do."

"Be candid with everyone."

**JACK WELCH**
*The legendary CEO of GE who grew the company by 4,000% during his tenure*

RUSH TO REVENUE
Money Cures All Problems

5. You struggle to hold your staff accountable to being on time because you worry about them saying, "TRAFFIC WAS TERRIBLE," "LOOK I GOT TO WORK AS SOON AS I COULD", "I FORGOT" or "I'M SO SORRY I OVERSLEPT." You actually have created a business where you feel as though your staff owns the business because they tell you what hours they will work and what jobs they are willing to do.

"Jesus entered the temple courts and drove out all who were buying and selling there. He overturned the tables of the money changers and the benches of those selling doves. "It is written," he said to them, "'My house will be called a house of prayer,' but you are making it 'a den of robbers."

**MATTHEW 21:12-13**

6. You struggle to raise prices to a profitable level, so you just slave away working hard without making a profit because you worry about what your customers will say.

"Sales are contingent upon the attitude of the salesman, not the attitude of the prospect."

**WILLIAM CLEMENT STONE**
*Best selling author and sales expert*

## LIVE WITHOUT BOUNDARIES

"Caring about what everybody thinks is bad for your mental health. Doing this will cause you live a life without boundaries and to dedicate your living hours to chasing the impossible goal of pleasing everybody, responding to every email, every text message, and offending no one. The key to being happy is getting yourself to a point where you are intentional about what and who you care about and being intentional about what you don't care about. Only after you have invested the time to determine your values and your goals related to your faith, family, friendships, fitness, fun, and finances will you be able to truly know what and who you should care about. My friend you must care about something. But you must only care about what truly matters. Your faith. Your family. Your friendships. Your fitness. Your fun. Your finances. Your New England Patriots. It's absolutely impossible to become a successful person without becoming the butt of the jokes made by your critics. To truly get to the place where you sincerely do not care about what most people think, you must firmly know your goals and where you are going with your life."

**CLAY TIBERIUS CLARK**
*The former U.S. SBA Entrepreneur of the Year, the father of the 5 human kids, the raiser of 40 chickens, and America's most pale male*

"Every sale has five basic obstacles: no need, no money, no hurry, no desire, no trust."

**ZIG ZIGLAR**
*Best selling author and sales expert*

"There is only one way to avoid criticism: do nothing, say nothing, and be nothing."

**ARISTOTLE**
*(The famous Greek philosopher)*

RUSH TO REVENUE
Money Cures All Problems

7. You struggle to get your staff to pay attention in meetings, to stop texting while at work, to stay off of their cell phones, and to stop updating their social media accounts during the work day because you worry about what "they" may say, when you call "them" out.

# You will Create Enemies if You are Honest

"You have enemies? Good. That means you've stood up for something sometime in your life."

**WINSTON CHURCHILL**
*The Prime Minister of the United Kingdom from 1940 to 1945 who lead the British in their fight against Adolf Hitler and Nazi Germany. He also led the country from 1951 to 1955. Churchill was an officer in the British Army, a non-academic historian, a writer (as Winston S. Churchill), and an artist. He won the Nobel Prize in Literature in 1953 for his overall, lifetime body of work.*

Put your focus on selling something or your bank
account will be empty like the page above.

# Dear Self,

This is my year to thrive in the F6 areas of my life. I realize that I have the power to design and live the life I want. I am committing here and now (Like the old school Luther Vandross song) to apply what I am learning at this workshop because I know that vision without execution is hallucination.

Sign Here: _____

Date: _____

**CHAPTER 1**

# DON'T FAKE IT

## THE SYSTEM ONLY WORKS IF YOU HAVE A REAL PRODUCT OR SERVICE

(Quit Trying to Get-Rich-Quick, Pump Up Your Ponzi-Scheme, or Make Millions While Putting No-Money Down... And Forget About 8-Minute Abs).

"ALL THE SMILES IN THE WORLD AREN'T GOING
TO HELP YOU IF YOUR PRODUCT OR SERVICE IS
NOT WHAT THE CUSTOMER WANTS."
"THE SERVICE PROFIT CHAIN"

I am writing this book because Dr. Zoellner and I want to teach YOU how to start and grow a sustainably successful business so that YOU can create both the financial and time freedom YOU need to enjoy YOUR life as you see fit. The only reason a business exists is to serve YOU and provide YOU with the funds to pursue YOUR F6 goals. If you had all of the money in the world, what would you spend your time doing? I know that I enjoy chasing my wife around and harassing our 5 kids. I enjoy artwork and cartooning. I enjoy burning stuff and obsessing about the New England Patriots. My friend, take this very moment and do something that only millionaires and successful people do, write down your goals and then I'll show you how to achieve them.

5 KIDS + 1 WIFE + 9 COMPANIES = BUSY LIFE

# RICH PEOPLE ARE INTENTIONAL ABOUT NOT WASTING TIME

88% of wealthy read 30 minutes or more each day for education or career reasons vs. 2% of poor.

80% of wealthy are focused on accomplishing some single goal. Only 12% of the poor do this.

84% of wealthy believe good habits create opportunity luck vs. 4% of poor.

86% of wealthy believe in lifelong educational self-improvment vs. 5% of poor.
richhabitsinstitute.com

"The goal is to create a business that will serve you."

**DOCTOR ROBERT ZOELLNER**

# DEEP THOUGHT:

If you build a business that doesn't serve you, what is the point?

# Define your why:

Why do you want to start or grow your business?

_____

How many deals per day do you need to achieve your life goal?

_____

## What are you willing to trade off for the success you seek?

- ☐ TV
- ☐ Social Media
- ☐ Sleep
- ☐ Disorganization
- ☐ Dysfunctional Relationships
- ☐ Fear of Rejection
- ☐ Savings
- ☐ Video Games

- ☐ _____
- ☐ _____
- ☐ _____

**BONUS FUN FACT**

We all only have 24 hours per day.

## WRITE YOUR GOALS HERE:

**WHEN WILL YOU PURSUE THESE GOALS?**

Faith Goals: _____ _____

Family Goals: _____ _____

Friendship Goals: _____ _____

Fitness Goals: _____ _____

Finance Goals: _____ _____

Fun Goals: _____ _____

We both grew up poor and between Doctor Zoellner and I, we have built (in no particular order) America's largest wedding entertainment company (www.DJConnection.com), two booming optometry clinics (www.DRZoellner.com), one of the most successful men's grooming (haircut) businesses in Oklahoma (www.EITRLounge.com), one of the largest auto auctions in the mid-west (Z66AA.com), the most successful PR and Marketing Firm in Oklahoma (www.MakeYourLifeEpic.com), a thriving durable medical company called A to Z Medical (www.AToZMedicaltulsa.com), the nation's largest award-winning wedding photography company (www.EpicPhotos.com), a bank (that Doctor Zoellner invested heavily in...www.BankRegent.com), a thriving online school (www.ThriveTimeShow.com), a regional radio show (www.ThriveTimeShow.com), and a 200 acre championship horse-breeding ranch (www.rockinzranchok.com). Building a successful business is not infinitely complicated, you just have to start by solving a problem that people legitimately have and that you can solve at a profit. Entrepreneurship is not about "going viral", "being disruptive in the marketplace," "success secrets," and all of the crap that you will learn if you earn an MBA, invest every waking hour into watching TED Talks, or spend your hard-earned money paying Tai Lopez or the countless other online charlatans who promise your instant success. By the way, Tai Lopez's office is located at the following address: Office 3, Unit R, Penfold Works Trading Estate Imperial Way, Watford, Herts, WD24 4YY. Do a search for his building using Google Maps. It's fascinating. ThriveTimeShow.com is located at 1100 Riverwalk Terrace #100 Jenks, OK, 74037.

"A Carnegie or a Rockefeller or a James J. Hill or a Marshall Field accumulates a fortune through the application of the same principles available to all of us, but we envy them and their wealth without ever thinking of studying their philosophy and applying it to ourselves. We look at a successful person in the hour of their triumph and wonder how they did it, but we overlook the importance of analyzing their methods and we forget the price they had to pay in the careful and well-organized preparation that had to be made before they could reap the fruits of their efforts."

**NAPOLEON HILL**
*Best-selling author of the #1 self-help book of all-time Think & Grow Rich, the personal apprentice of the late great Andrew Carnegie, and a mentor of Oral Roberts.*

"One way to get priorities accomplished is to schedule them into your calender."

**LEE COCKERELL**
*(THE FORMER EXECUTIVE VICE PRESIDENT OF WALT DISNEY WORLD RESORTS)*

RUSH TO REVENUE
Money Cures All Problems

# REAL THRIVERS LIKE YOU

"Clay, you have helped me from day one to be a better leader of my family and my business through the passion you bring to both! Thank you, sir. I've applied some of the philosophies from your awesome book, Make Your Life Epic to my LegalShield business and they have helped me achieve the top spot in the state...THANK YOU for your leadership."

*Robert Johnson | Legal Shield*

Entrepreneurship is about diligent doers solving people's problems. People are willing to pay diligent doers to effectively and efficiently solve their problems. Once you find that product or service that people are willing to pay for, then all you have to do is build a scalable system and hold your team accountable to profitability by executing your repeatable system over and over and over...And the process of holding yourself and your team accountable to the execution of business systems requires the constant application of effort (diligence).

**Diligence**
Earnest and persistent application of effort.

"Lazy hands make for poverty, but diligent hands bring wealth."

**PROVERBS 10:4**

## The Boring Stuff Matters Most

"I have learned from both my own successes and failures and those of many others that it's the boring stuff that matters the most. Startup success is not a consequence of good genes or being in the right place at the right time. Startup success can be engineered by following the right process, which means it can be learned, which means it can be taught."

**ERIC RIES**
*Best-selling author of the Lean Startup and former consultant at Kleiner Perkins*

*"People think focus means saying yes to the thing you've got to focus on. But that's not what it means at all. It means saying no to the hundred other good ideas that there are. You have to pick carefully. I'm actually as proud of the things we haven't done as the things I have done. Innovation is saying no to 1,000 things."*
- Steve Jobs, Founder of Apple and former CEO of Pixar

## "The Diligent Doer"

A. Knows their "why".
B. Knows their daily Key Performance Indicators.
C. Uses one weekly meeting to work on their business; to discuss their problems and produce systematic solutions.
D. Assigns detailed and granular action times (who, what, when, why) items
E. Follows up. Builds accountability.
F. Insists on organization and proper nomenclature.

VS

*"Most people are sitting on their own diamond mines. The surest ways to lose your diamond mine are to get bored, become overambitious, or start thinking that the grass is greener on the other side. Find your core focus, stick to it, and devote your time and resources to excelling at it." - Gino Wickman, Traction: Get a Grip on Your Business*

## "The Happy Hoper"

A. Not committed to their "why".
B. Focuses on creating many new ideas, not the execution of previous ideas.
C. Uses endless emails, texts, meetings, and calls to discuss their individual burning fires.
D. Assigns vague, general concepts and ideas without details.
E. Allows people to make them feel bad about holding others accountable.
F. Insists on disorganization and the absence of nomenclature.

*"Most entrepreneurs are merely technicians with an entrepreneurial seizure. Most entrepreneurs fail because you are working IN your business rather than ON your business." - Michael Gerber, Bestselling author of E-Myth*

---

During this book, I will teach you the 13-point success system that Dr. Z and I have made and personally implemented in our own lives and businesses, but the system will not work if you do not have a real product or service that the world really wants. To create time and financial freedom intentionally make trade offs. What will you be willing to give up?

---

- TV
- Social Media
- Negative Relationships
- Sleep
- Distractions
- Social Events

# SO WHAT HAPPENS IF YOU STRUGGLE TO GET THINGS DONE?

Developing the habits of diligence and consistency are just like developing physical muscles. These small little wins and these small little victories where you get to cross an item off of the to-do list that you made, are at the very core of successful entrepreneurship. However, if you find yourself consistently dropping the ball and failing to get things done, you need to correct this behavior immediately. And because you are self-employed, you cannot really fire yourself without going into bankruptcy, so failure is not an option and this is how you avoid it.

"Strength & Growth come only through continuous effort & struggle."

**NAPOLEON HILL**

# THE PLAYS FOR AVOIDING FAILURE

1.  Ask yourself why you did not get it done.

2.  Determine what tools, coaching, and resources you need to have access to before attempting to start each action step.

3.  Determine how long it's going to realistically take to get the action item done.

4.  Determine where you need to physically be to focus and concentrate on the task at hand long enough to complete the action item.

5.  Determine specifically when you are going to knock out the action item.

6.  Determine if you really do believe that completing this action item will help you grow your business to truly create both the time and financial freedom you seek.

7.  Determine whether you are truly open to correction and coaching in this area or if this is just something that you are simply not going to do.

Are you suffering from Monkey Brain?

RUSH TO REVENUE
Money Cures All Problems

"The way to get started is to quit talking and begin doing."

**WALT DISNEY**
*Legendary animator, award-winning writer, producer, film-maker and the man who created the Walt Disney empire*

"People think focus means saying yes to the thing you've got to focus on. But that's not what it means at all. It means saying no to the hundred other good ideas that there are. You have to pick carefully. I'm actually as proud of the things we haven't done as the things I have done. Innovation is saying no to 1,000 things."

**STEVE JOBS**
*Co-founder of Apple and the former CEO of PIXAR*

"Render more service than that which you are paid and you will soon be paid for more than you render. The law of increasing returns takes care of this."

"In every soul there has been deposited the seed of a great future, but that seed will never germinate, much less grow to maturity, except through the rendering of useful service."

**NAPOLEON HILL**
*Best-selling author of the #1 self-help book of all-time Think & Grow Rich, the personal apprentice of the late great Andrew Carnegie and a mentor of Oral Roberts*

If you are trying to GET-RICH-QUICK by pitching a dysfunctional scheme based upon a smoke-and-mirrors product that doesn't work (but was independently tested in some unverifiable European lab) or to make your millions by betting on the false hope of buying the failing currencies of third-world nations for pennies on the dollar, then this system is not going to work and in fact, no system will work because you are attempting to violate a universal law you and I cannot change, circumvent, or rush past.

"*ENTREPRENEURS SOLVE THE WORLD'S PROBLEMS AND UNAPOLOGETICALLY MAKE MONEY DOING IT.*"
*- CLAY CLARK, FOUNDER OF THRIVE15*

"Dishonest money dwindles away, but whoever gathers money little by little makes it grow."

**PROVERBS 13:11**
*From the controversial book called The Bible*

Success is achieved as a result of scalably offering the world a solution to one of their problems in exchange for the money that you desire.

YOUR BUSINESS EXISTS TO SOLVE PROBLEMS
FOR YOU AND YOUR CUSTOMERS.
- CLAY CLARK
FOUNDER OF THRIVE15

- **Steve Jobs** provided the world with computers that the average human could actually use.

- **Henry Ford** made it affordable for humans to travel freely throughout the country.

- **Russell Simmons** introduced the world to beats, rhythms, and rap music they had never heard of.

- **Justin Timberlake** entertains us and makes us laugh with his musical, comedic, and acting skills.

- **Larry Page** and **Sergey Brin** made it possible for us to quickly find the answers to our problems by just typing something into a search bar.

- **Andrew Carnegie** teamed up with Henry Bessemer to make the manufacturing of steel efficient and affordable.

- **Dr. Zoellner** provides Tulsa with affordable eye glasses, contacts, and eye care.

- **I, Clay Clark,** made quality wedding entertainment both consistent and affordable.

- **You,** _____(your name), will provide _____ (solution, service, product, what?) in exchange for _____ (the riches that you seek?).

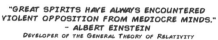

"GREAT SPIRITS HAVE ALWAYS ENCOUNTERED VIOLENT OPPOSITION FROM MEDIOCRE MINDS."
– ALBERT EINSTEIN
DEVELOPER OF THE GENERAL THEORY OF RELATIVITY

# WHAT PROBLEMS CAN YOU SOLVE FOR YOUR IDEAL AND LIKELY BUYERS?

Bottom line: the first step you must take to start a successful business is to solve real problems that real humans have in exchange for real money. If you already have customers because you are already solving problems for real humans, I STRONGLY encourage you to make a list of all of the problems that your IDEAL AND LIKELY BUYERS have and what products and services you could offer to them to help provide them solutions:

| Problem | Solution |
|---------|----------|
| | |
| | |
| | |
| | |
| | |
| | |
| | |
| | |
| | |
| | |
| | |
| | |
| | |
| | |
| | |
| | |
| | |
| | |

Story Time:

1. You and me meeting clients in the dark,

2. Danzig, Mother and the mother of the bride.

"DON'T LET SCHOOLING INTERFERE WITH YOUR EDUCATION."
- MARK TWAIN, AMERICAN AUTHOR

# 6 SUPERPLAYS FOR CREATING A PRODUCT OR SERVICE PEOPLE WILL LOVE.

1. Make all aspects of your product or service appealing (menus, packaging, decor, etc.)

2. Make all aspects of your business appealing to the ears.

3. Make all aspects of your business great tasting.

4. Script every interaction point with your customers.

5. Over deliver and soon you will be overpaid.

6. Systematically gather feedback from your ideal and likely buyers.

> "BE LIKE A POSTAGE STAMP.
> STICK TO IT UNTIL YOU GET THERE."
> –HARVEY MACKAY
> ENTREPRENEUR, MOTIVATIONAL SPEAKER AND AUTHOR

DETER MEND
MEDIOCRITY PL.
NOWHERE, UTAH

CLAY CLARK
777 SUCCESS AVE.
74119 TULSA, OK

*Claymations*

---

Quit trying to get rich quick and get started becoming rich as a result of diligence over time.

---

"You can have everything in life you want, if you will just help other people get what they want."

**ZIG ZIGLAR**
*Motivational speaker and best-selling author*

## PRO-TIPS FROM PROVERBS

Dishonest money dwindles away, but whoever gathers money little by little makes it grow. **Proverbs 13:11**

Lazy hands make for poverty, but diligent hands bring wealth. **Proverbs 10:4**

The soul of the sluggard craves and gets nothing, while the soul of the diligent is richly supplied. **Proverbs 13:4**

## APPLE
## THE "OVERNIGHT SUCCESS"

It took the now mythological entrepreneur, Steve Jobs, nearly two decades to become an overnight billionaire. He founded the company in his parents' garage in Cupertino, California, in 1976. His company really did not develop any significant traction until it created the Macintosh in 1984, which was eight years later. The company spent the entire 80s and 90s struggling to gain market share, but they finally made it once they invented the iMac and other consumer products **It only took Steve Jobs eight years to "make it big."**

RUSH TO REVENUE
Money Cures All Problems

# REAL THRIVERS LIKE YOU

"Our experience working with Clay Clark and his team has been nothing short of amazing. When our team first met Clay, I expressed that if we were able to move the needle and get results, we would be working together for a very long time. Clay and his team listened to our problems and custom built a program specifically for us. So far this season, we have experienced a 42% increase in corporate sponsorship sales, a 10% increase in season ticket sales and over a 103% increase in group tickets sales! We have also had a 21% increase in people actually attending the games thus resulting in a 27% increase in concession and novelty sales. Our program focused on search engine optimization, an increased social media presence, targeted online ads, digital retargeting ads, and the implementation of the Dream 100 system. Beyond that, Clay's team redesigned our website making it more visually appealing and user friendly for our online visitors by creating a dynamic visual experience. Our slogan for Tulsa Oilers hockey is 'Feel The Boom'; thanks Clay for giving us that BOOM!"

*Taylor Hall | Tulsa Oilers | General Manager*
*www.tulsaoilers.com*

## GOOGLE
## THE "OVERNIGHT SUCCESS"

In 1996, Sergey Brin and Larry Page began investing both their time and money into what is now known as Google. Originally, the project was called Backrub with a stated goal of attempting to index and download the entire Internet. In 1999, most humans had never heard of the search engine, and almost no one was using it. However, after several business development deals and five additional years of hard work, Google achieved success and went public in 2004 with a market capitalization of 24 billion.

**They became rich quick after investing 8 years in building the company.**

## FEDEX
## THE "OVERNIGHT SUCCESS"

Fred Smith first had the "BIG IDEA" to start FedEX in 1962. He sketched out his business plan while attending Yale University. However, it took Fred 9 years and until 1971 to turn his "BIG IDEA" into a profitable business.

---

**Would it really be nice? Would it really be nice to focus on the same thing for 7 years before "making it big?"**

---

RUSH TO REVENUE
Money Cures
All Problems

## ESPN
## THE "OVERNIGHT SUCCESS"

The father-and-son combo of Bill and Scott
Rasmussen had the "BIG IDEA" to team up
with the AETNA insurance agent Ed Eagan to
launch the world's first all sports network in
1978. However, after launching the network
on September 7, 1979, at 7 p.m. Eastern Time,
their "BIG IDEA" did not produce a profit
until the mid-80s.

★ ★ ★ ★ ★

# REAL THRIVERS LIKE YOU

"I own Facchianos Bridal and Formal attire and have had to pay thousands of dollars in the past to have websites built that were subpar and not what I needed for my business, until Clay taught me how to do it myself. Now my company website comes up on the search engines in the first three searches. It has changed my business overnight on how many times our phone rings. It can change the life of your business to be in control of your website."

*Jennifer Thompson | Owner/Bridal Stylist | Facchianos Bridal and Formal Attire*

## ELEPHANT IN THE ROOM
## THE "OVERNIGHT SUCCESS"

My brother-in-law and I started the Elephant In The Room Men's Grooming Lounge at 1609 South Boston. The entire team consisted of both he and I working together and the entire business was funded with our personal cash. To bring in initial customers to "test our system on", we

promoted the business directly through my Facebook contacts, Justin's Facebook contacts, and a door-to-door marketing effort that involved him personally walking from business to business passing out "GET A FREE HAIRCUT" cards to people. The homeless community loved those cards and so did about one out of ten people that we passed those cards out to. Now store number three at 1660 North 9th Street in Broken Arrow is thriving, and we are in the process of relocating our 1609 South Boston store to accommodate the growth. We are also finishing plans for the opening of our fourth store.

**Our overnight success came on year four of operations.**

# FOCUS ON CREATING A REAL BUSINESS.

"Pyramid schemes now come in so many forms that they may be difficult to recognize immediately. However, they all share one overriding characteristic. They promise consumers or investors large profits based primarily on recruiting others to join their program, not based on profits from any real investment or real sale of goods to the public. Some schemes may purport to sell a product, but they often simply use the product to hide their pyramid structure. There are two tell-tale signs that a product is simply being used to disguise a pyramid scheme: inventory loading and a lack of retail sales. Inventory loading occurs when a company's incentive program forces recruits to buy more products than they could ever sell, often at inflated prices. If this occurs throughout the company's distribution system, the people at the top of the pyramid reap substantial profits, even though little or no product moves to market. The people at the bottom make excessive payments for inventory that simply accumulates in their basements. A lack of retail sales is also a red flag that a pyramid exists. Many pyramid schemes will claim that their product is selling like hot cakes. However, on closer examination, the sales occur only between people inside the pyramid structure or to new recruits joining the structure, not to consumers out in the general public."

**DEBRA A. VALENTINE**
*Former General Counsel at the Federal Trade Commission*

*https://www.ftc.gov/public-statements/1998/05/pyramid-schemes*

# WHEN PYRAMID SCHEMES BLOW UP

**DEC. 15, 2015**

Vemma Agrees to Ban on Pyramid Scheme Practices in order to Settle FTC Charges - health drinks marketer touted unlimited income potential, but most people lost money

*https://www.ftc.gov/news-events/press-releases/2016/12/vemma-agrees-ban-pyramid-scheme-practices-settle-ftc-charges*

**NOV. 8, 2016**

FTC Returns More Than $3.7 Million to People Harmed by Pyramid Scheme

*https://www.ftc.gov/news-events/press-releases/2016/11/ftc-returns-more-37-million-people-harmed-pyramid-scheme*

**JUNE 14, 2016**

FTC Sending Refund Checks Totaling More Than $9 Million to Consumers Who Bought Pure Health or Genesis Today Green Coffee Weight-Loss Supplements

*https://www.ftc.gov/news-events/press-releases/2016/06/ftc-sending-refund-checks-totaling-more-9-million-consumers-who*

"Both Ponzi schemes and pyramids are quite seductive because they may be able to deliver a high rate of return to a few early investors for a short period of time. Yet, both pyramid and Ponzi schemes are illegal because they inevitably must fall apart. No program can recruit new members forever. Every pyramid or Ponzi scheme collapses because it cannot expand beyond the size of the earth's population. When the scheme collapses, most investors find themselves at the bottom, unable to recoup their losses."

**DEBRA A. VALENTINE**
*Former General Counsel at the Federal Trade Commission*

*https://www.ftc.gov/public-statements/1998/05/pyramid-schemes*

RUSH TO REVENUE
Money Cures All Problems

"Here are some telltale signs of a pyramid scheme — think of these as "Spotting an Illegal Pyramid Scheme 101."

1. **Recruit, recruit, recruit.** If your income is based predominantly on how many people you recruit into the program, not how much product you sell, it's a pyramid scheme. According to the FTC's complaint, Vemma's marketing and training materials emphasize recruiting other Affiliates. In fact, one of the masterminds behind the alleged scheme says Affiliates should focus on recruiting other Affiliates because customers are simply a "byproduct of the business."

2. **Buy our product, lots of it.** Many pyramid scheme operations require participants to buy the product or other things to stay in good standing with the company. Vemma Affiliates are told to spend 150 bucks a month on products to stay in the monthly "bonus" pool, according to the complaint. That's $1,800 a year!

3. **Live the lavish lifestyle.** The recruitment pitch says you'll be living in the lap of luxury. It fails to tell you most people in a pyramid scheme lose money. Vemma made promises of luxury cars and travel to exotic destinations, but the company's own income disclosures tell a different story: 9 out of 10 Affiliates made less than $6,200. And the FTC alleges even those figures are overblown because they don't take into account expenses like the initial purchase and the monthly purchases."

**ALVARO PUIG**
*Consumer Education Specialist at the Federal Trade Commission*

*https://www.consumer.ftc.gov/blog/spotting-illegal-pyramid-scheme-101*

## Quit trying to make millions while putting no money down in real estate.

# GET RICH QUICK = GO BROKE FAST

John Nelson Beck ran infomercials peddling a real estate system that promised purchasers easy money buying foreclosed homes at government auctions and flipping them or putting them up for rent. John Beck's Free & Clear Real Estate System" cost $39.95, plus shipping and handling, and came with written materials, CDs and DVDs, the Times reported. In 2012, the FTC obtained a $479 million judgment against Beck and the other defendants. Beck was ordered to personally pay $113 million.

*http://www.foxnews.com/us/2016/02/13/california-man-vanishes-owing-ftc-113-million-over-get-rich-quick-scam.html*

"IF YOU WANT TO SAVE YOURSELF A BUNCH OF TIME, IT IS ALWAYS EASIER TO BE A PIRATE THAN A PIONEER."
- CLAY CLARK, FOUNDER OF THRIVE15

# WHAT SOLUTION WILL YOU PROVIDE THE WORLD IN EXCHANGE FOR THE MONEY YOU SEEK?

1. Invest the time needed to find and solve a problem that consumers have and are willing to pay for.

2. Invest as much time as needed until you find an existing product or service that you could compete within the marketplace in a differentiated way.

## What Problems Can You Solve?

_____

_____

_____

_____

_____

_____

## With What Product or Service Can You Compete?

_____

_____

_____

_____

_____

_____

_____

RUSH TO REVENUE
Money Cures All Problems

# When Scammers Get Busted

## TV pitchman Kevin Trudeau sentenced to 10 years in prison

March 17, 2014 | By Jason Meisner | Tribune reporter

When TV huckster Kevin Trudeau stood in a packed federal courtroom to make one final sales pitch Monday, he hardly resembled the tanned, dapper figure seen hawking miracle diets and natural cancer cures ⬀ on so many late-night infomercials.

Television pitchman Kevin Trudeau leaves the Dirksen U.S. Court...

After spending four months in jail for contempt of court, Trudeau's trademark jet black coif was thin and gray. His usual tailored suit was replaced by rumpled orange jail clothes. Even his typical air ⬀ of defiance had turned to contrition, a change he said washed over him during his sleepless first night in custody.

*http://articles.chicagotribune.com/2014-03-17/business/chi-kevin-trudeau-sentenced-20140317_1_kevin-trudeau-global-information-network-guzman*

> "The quality of service you render, PLUS the quantity of service you render, PLUS the mental attitude in which you render service DETERMINES the space you occupy in your chosen calling AND the compensation you get from your services."

**NAPOLEON HILL**
*Best-selling author of the #1 self-help book of all-time Think & Grow Rich, the personal apprentice of the late great Andrew Carnegie, and a mentor of Oral Roberts*

> "Kevin Trudeau's run-ins with the FTC began back in the late 90's when he agreed to settle an FTC charge that he hosted a series of deceptive infomercials designed to look like radio and TV news interviews. But Trudeau didn't change his ways after the settlement. Instead, he claimed in a new infomercial – without any proof – that "Coral Calcium Supreme" could treat or cure cancer and other diseases. In 2004, the FTC had him banned from infomercials. But Trudeau used a narrow exception in the ban to promote a new item: a book about a weight loss plan..."

**ANDREW JOHNSON**
*Division of Consumer and Business Education, FTC*

*Excerpt from "Refunds for Kevin Trudeau's Victims"*
*https://www.consumer.ftc.gov/blog/refunds-kevin-trudeaus-victims*

> "If you can't sell your business will go to Hell."

**CLAY TIBERIUS CLARK**

 Story Time:

1 community fridge, yogurt deposits, brownie withdrawls, and fun with laxatives.

Hear Clay's Story in Person @ the Thrive Conference

RUSH TO REVENUE
Money Cures All Problems

# THE PLAYS FOR AVOIDING SUCCESS

1. Likes

2. Clicks

3. Funnels

4. Impressions

5. Products "They don't want you to know about."

6. Viral Social Media Marketing Plans

7. Pop-Up Get-Rich-Quick Schemes

8. Subscription-Based Education Programs

9. Ideas

10. Movements / Causes

11. Products that have not been proven to work:

12. Certifications for training / coaching

# CHAPTER 2

# SOWING & REAPING

## THE LAW OF CAUSE AND EFFECT

RUSH TO REVENUE
Money Cures All Problems

"IF YOU'RE GOING TO BE THINKING ANYTHING,
YOU MIGHT AS WELL THINK BIG."
– DONALD TRUMP
REAL ESTATE DEVELOPER, MOGUL, BILLIONAIRE, AND 45TH PRESIDENT
OF THE UNITED STATES

## BONUS TIP:

Call all of your leads every day until they cry, die, or buy.

As a general rule, the universal law of cause and effect is understood as the law that states for every effect there is a definite cause. Essentially, if you don't till the right piece of land, till the land properly, plant the corn correctly, and water the corn diligently, it won't grow.

## MOST BUSINESSES FAIL BY DEFAULT

According to Inc. Magazine, 96% of Businesses Fail Within 10 Years.

*http://www.inc.com/bill-carmody/why-96-of-businesses-fail-within-10-years.html*

- If you don't implement our proven system to help you clarify your revenue goals, you will lose in the game of business.

- If you don't invest the time to discover the number of customers you need to break-even, you will be flying blind and you will lose.

- If you don't talk to your significant other or yourself about your work / life balance, boundaries, and the total number of hours you are willing to work each week on your business, you will have problems at home like I did before I was taught the proven time management systems by Doctor Zoellner, Mr. Terry Fisher, and the former Executive Vice President of Walt Disney World Resorts and my friend, Lee Cockerell

"Find experts to assist you in areas you are not strong in."

"Until you value yourself, you will not value your time. Until you value your time, you will not do anything with it."

**LEE COCKERELL**
*Thrive15.com Partner and Mentor and the former Executive Vice President of Walt Disney World Resorts who used to manage 40,000 cast members / employees*

## Till
To prepare (soil, a piece of land, etc.) for growing crops.

RUSH TO REVENUE
Money Cures All Problems

- If you don't determine your unique value proposition, your marketing efforts will not produce fruit. If you don't improve your branding and focus on creating a world-class brand, you will not be taken seriously by your ideal and likely buyers.

- If you don't invest the time to create a 3-legged marketing stool like Doctor Zoellner has done at Robert Zoellner and Associates (www.DrZoellner.com), your business will struggle to consistently gain new customers year after year.

"EVERYTHING ELSE BECOMES UNNECESSARY IN A BUSINESS IF NOBODY SELLS ANYTHING."
- CLAY CLARK, FOUNDER OF THRIVE15

"Hire salespeople who are really smart problem solvers, but lack courage, hunger and competitiveness, and your company will go out of business."

**BEN HOROWITZ**
*An American businessman, investor, blogger, and author. He is a high technology entrepreneur and co-founder and general partner along with Marc Andreessen of the venture capital firm Andreessen Horowitz. He co-founded and served as president and chief executive officer of the enterprise software company Opsware, which Hewlett-Packard acquired for $1.6 billion in cash in July 2007)*

- If you don't implement a proven sales conversion system, you are going to go into bankruptcy or you are going to have to work two jobs until the end of your life. The reason why my wedding-related businesses, www.DJConnection.com and www.EpicPhotos.com, did so well was not because of my vast knowledge of weddings or my super skills when it came to taking wedding photographs. In fact, I didn't even know how to take wedding photos when we started the company and I still didn't know how to take wedding photos when I sold it.

The reason why these businesses thrived was because I knew how to solve the problems experienced by brides and grooms and I built a repeatable process that allowed us to sell thousands upon thousands of wedding packages year after year... and **YOU CAN LEARN THESE SYSTEMS TOO!**

- If you don't invest the time that most people spend watching television and mindlessly interacting on social media to determine your sustainable customers acquisition costs, you are not going to be able to fund the growth of your business. Why does the Z66 Auto Auction (www.Z66AA.com) dominate the Tulsa marketplace? Is it because Dr. Zoellner has an obsession with tinkering with cars or because he is passionate about automobiles? No. This business and all of his businesses dominate because he knows how to implement and adapt these best-practice systems into nearly every industry on the planet. Although, we have never tried to get involved in the petting-zoo industry.

## THE AVERAGE AMERICAN WATCHES OVER 5 HOURS OF TV PER DAY.

"On average, American adults are watching five hours and four minutes of television per day. The bulk of that — about four and a half hours of it — is live television, which is television watched when originally broadcast. Thirty minutes more comes via DVR."

*"How Much Do We Love TV? Let Us Count the Ways," John Koblin, June 30th 2016, New York Times*

"Teens spend 9 hours a day, tweens 6 hours a day on average consuming media, report discovers."

*"Teens Spend a 'Mind-Boggling' 9 Hours a Day Using Media, Report Says," Kelly Wallace, CNN*

RUSH TO REVENUE
Money Cures All Problems

# REAL THRIVERS LIKE YOU

"Clay is very engaging, very charming and very humorous and his presentation had a very practical side too. As a speaker, he teaches you things that you can use to make yourself more successful and your business more successful. But perhaps more significantly, he has that genuine enthusiasm. After I listened to his presentation, it was like an emotional springboard. It was one of the best presentations I've ever seen. I've seen Jack Canfield and I've seen Tony Robbins, and I can tell you that Clay made a far greater impact on me than any of those other speakers, as great as they are and as great as they were at that time."

*Lance Dawson | Mortgage Broker | www.mortgagearchitects.ca*

- If you don't invest the hours needed to actually get out a whiteboard and write out and create repeatable business systems, processes, and a consistent file nomenclature system, you will have a dysfunctional company where nobody can find anything, you work all of the time, and you are essentially building a job that nobody wants instead of a business that has the power to provide you with time and financial freedom.

"MAKE A PLACE FOR EVERYTHING."
-CLAY CLARK
FOUNDER OF THRIVE15

## When Will You Make the Time To Work on Your Business?

"A Level Two business is a business that works, but only because you, the business owner, are there every day to make it work. You make most of the decisions. You generate most of the business. You meet with all the key clients and perform most of the important work of the business...The painful reality is that most Level Two business owners get caught in the "Self" Employment Trap. They're so busy doing the "job" of their business that they can't step back and focus on growing their business. What's more, because of the way they are building their business, the more success they have, the more trapped they become inside their company."

**JEFF HOFFMAN & DAVID FINKEL**
*Authors of the best-selling book Scale and the former CEO of Priceline*

RUSH TO REVENUE
Money Cures All Problems

- If you don't implement the proven management systems that we are going to teach you, you are going to create a business that is in charge of you and a team of employees who get to work and tell you what they are going to do every day. Pretty soon, you'll start to feel like they are the ones that own the business because they are the ones that are calling all of the shots.

"Every time I read a management or self-help book, I find myself saying, "That's fine, but that wasn't really the hard thing about the situation." The hard thing isn't setting a big, hairy, audacious goal. The hard thing is laying people off when you miss the big goal. The hard thing isn't hiring great people. The hard thing is when those "great people" develop a sense of entitlement and start demanding unreasonable things. The hard thing isn't setting up an organizational chart. The hard thing is getting people to communicate within the organization that you just designed. The hard thing isn't dreaming big. The hard thing is waking up in the middle of the night in a cold sweat when the dream turns into a nightmare."

**BEN HOROWITZ**
*An American businessman, investor, blogger, and author. He is a high technology entrepreneur and co-founder and general partner along with Marc Andreessen of the venture capital firm Andreessen Horowitz. He co-founded and served as president and chief executive officer of the enterprise software company Opsware, which Hewlett-Packard acquired for $1.6 billion in cash in July 2007*

"THE LOWER AN INDIVIDUAL'S ABILITY TO LEAD, THE LOWER THE LID ON HIS POTENTIAL."
- JOHN MAXWELL
AMERICAN AUTHOR, SPEAKER, AND PASTOR

- If you don't create a sustainable and repetitive weekly schedule, you will become overwhelmed, stressed out, and financially rich yet too exhausted to enjoy your earnings and the pursuit of your F6 goals.

"You either pay now or pay later with just about every decision you make about where and how you spend your time."

**LEE COCKERELL**
*Thrive15.com partner and mentor and the former Executive Vice President of Operations for Walt Disney World Resorts and the 40,000 team members that worked there*

- If you don't implement the proven human resources and recruitment systems that we'll teach you, you will become one of those sad entrepreneurs that runs around telling everybody that it's impossible to hire and retain good people. Then you'll eventually get into some small business networking group that validates your belief that it's impossible to hire good people these days.

LORD GRATHMA PROMISES THAT AFTER DEATH WE WILL ALL BURN IN ETERNAL FLAME UNTIL HIS HELL HOUNDS FINISH FEEDING OFF OUR DECOMPOSING FLESH. I WANT YOU TO JOIN ME IN PRAISING HIM FOR HIS GENEROSITY

THIS MESSAGE IS ENCOURAGING

"IT'S NEVER THE PLATFORM. IT'S ALWAYS THE MESSAGE."
- GARY VAYNERCHUK
CO-FOUNDER AND CEO OF A SOCIAL MEDIA BRAND CONSULTING AGENCY

# 75% OF EMPLOYEES STEAL

"The U.S. Chamber of Commerce estimates that 75% of employees steal from the workplace and that most do so repeatedly."

*"Employee Theft: Are You Blind to It?," Rich Russakoff and Mary Goodman, CBS News*

- If you don't implement the systematic step-by-step accounting coaching and systems that we will teach you, you will find that you are asking yourself rhetorically, "where did all of my money go?"

"A budget is telling your money where to go instead of wondering where it went."

**DAVE RAMSEY**
*Best-selling author, personal finance guru, and nationally syndicated talk-show host*

- Our ThriveTimeShow.com team will show you how to get to the top of Google for any given search term, but if you are not willing to write the pages and pages of original content needed to get to the top of the Google search engine and if you aren't willing to pay someone else to do it either, then your new knowledge about how to get to the top of Google is not going to help you. My friend, in the world of business, you and I get paid based upon what we get done not based upon what we know or how many degrees we have. The world of business is brutal in that it only rewards results and not intentions, memorization skill, or your ability to score high on tests.

"You don't get paid for the hour. You get paid for the value you bring to the hour."

**JIM ROHN**
*Best-selling author and legendary sales trainer / motivational speaker*

- Our ThriveTimeShow.com team will teach you how to market your business, how to build a sales conversion system, how to build a customer service experience checklist, how to become an excellent manager, how to manage your finances, how to hire top talent, how to get featured in media outlets, and every other thing that you need to know to be able to build a successful business, but you still have to execute and get things done either by doing it yourself or by hiring someone else to do it for you and it's going to require time to get things done.

# WHAT DOES "BOOM" MEAN?

If you listen to the ThriveTime Radio Show, if you come to the ThriveTimeShow.com World Headquarters, or if you spend any time on ThriveTimeShow.com, you will notice people all around you saying the phrase, "BOOM." So what does B.O.O.M. stand for? For Dr. Z and I, it stands for the big overwhelming optimistic momentum it takes to start and grow a successful business. All the practical business knowledge in the world is not going to help you to achieve success if you are not willing to bring BIG OVERWHELMING OPTIMISTIC MOMENTUM to the workplace on a daily basis.

## BOOM!

"Ideas are easy, implementation is hard."

**GUY KAWASAKI**
*American marketing specialist, author, and Silicon Valley venture capitalist. He was one of the Apple employees originally responsible for marketing their Macintosh computer line in 1984*

"Vision without execution is hallucination."

**THOMAS EDISON**
*The man credited as being the founder of GE, and the inventor of the first modern light bulb, recorded sound, and recorded audio*

RUSH TO REVENUE
Money Cures All Problems

So if you have to work so hard, what is the point of having a mentor, a coach, or an online school to show you the way? Because everybody needs a coach to push them to be their best and to help keep them headed down the right path. Without a mentor and a coach showing you the proven tough path up the mountain to success, you are going to have to learn exclusively from costly mistakes and that is why 90% of startups fail according to Forbes.

**MOST BUSINESSES FAIL BY DEFAULT**

**"90% Of Startups Fail"**

*"90% Of Startups Fail: Here's What You Need To Know About The 10%," Neil Patel, Forbes Magazine, January 16th, 2015*

DON'T FOLLOW THE TOURIST:
FOLLOW THE KING OF THE MOUNTAIN

HEY MISTER, HOW DO YOU CLIMB A MOUNTAIN?

Ummm...

# Find Someone Who Knows the Path

"The advice that sticks out I got from John Doerr, who in 2001 said, "My advice to you is to have a coach." The coach he said I should have is Bill Campbell. I initially resented the advice, because after all, I was a CEO. I was pretty experienced. Why would I need a coach? Am I doing something wrong? My argument was, How could a coach advise me if I'm the best person in the world at this? But that's not what a coach does. The coach doesn't have to play the sport as well as you do. They have to watch you and get you to be your best. In the business context, a coach is not a repetitious coach. A coach is somebody who looks at something with another set of eyes, describes it to you in [his] words, and discusses how to approach the problem.

Once I realized I could trust him and that he could help me with perspective, I decided this was a great idea. When there is [a] business conflict you tend to get rat-holed into it. [Bill's] general advice has been to rise one step higher, above the person on the other side of the table, and to take the long view. He'll say, "You're letting it bother you. Don't."

**ERIC SCHMIDT**
*Chairman and CEO of Google*

# STEVE JOBS THINKS I NEED A COACH?

The system that we are about to teach you works over and over again in every industry that we've owned businesses in and coached clients like you in, but you must commit to being a "diligent doer" and you cannot drift into becoming a "happy hoper."

> "He that walketh with wise men shall be wise, but a companion of fools shall be destroyed."

**PROVERBS 13:20**

> "That's been one of my mantras: focus and simplicity. Simple can be harder than complex."

**STEVE JOBS**
*The co-founder of Apple and the former CEO of PIXAR*

## FUN FACT

The number of NBA Championships won by Michael Jordan without legendary Coach Phil Jackson: 0

The number of NBA Championships won by Kobe Bryant without legendary Coach Phil Jackson: 0

> "Brevity is the soul of wit."

**WILLIAM SHAKESPEARE**
*The legendary playwright*

RUSH TO REVENUE
Money Cures All Problems

## LIST YOUR CURRENT BIGGEST LIMITING FACTORS

"The majority of people begin to drift as soon as they meet with opposition, and not one out of ten thousand (people) will keep on trying after failing two or three times."

**NAPOLEON HILL**
*The best-selling author of Think & Grow Rich and the personal apprentice of the world's second wealthiest man during his lifetime, Andrew Carnegie*

"The missing ingredient for nearly all of the 1,000-plus clients I have worked with directly to improve their businesses is pigheaded discipline and determination. We all get good ideas at seminars and from books, radio talk shows and business-building gurus. The problem is that most companies do not know how to identify and adapt the best ideas to their businesses. Implementation, not ideas, is the key to real success."

**CHET HOLMES**
*Former business partner of billionaire Charlie Munger and the best-selling author of The Ultimate Sales Machine*

RUSH TO REVENUE
*Money Cures All Problems*

# SCHEDULE YOUR SUCCESS

**Write down a list of ways that you are willing to market your business consistently and affordably:**

_____

_____

_____

_____

**Add into your schedule the time needed to sow the seeds in the following areas of your life:**

Faith: _____

Family: _____

Friendships: _____

Fitness: _____

Finances: _____

Fun: _____

**Invest as much time as needed until you find an existing product or service that you can compete with in the marketplace in a differentiated way.**

CHAPTER 3

# STEP 1
## ESTABLISH REVENUE GOALS

"The goal of your business is to serve you."

**DOCTOR ROBERT ZOELLNER**
*Optometrist turned multimillionaire and the CEO of Thrive15.com*

You mean entrepreneurs have to sit down and do math? But the reason you started a business was to avoid doing things that you don't like doing.

**WITHOUT PROPER GUIDANCE MOST BUSINESSES FAIL**

**"8 out of 10 entrepreneurs who start businesses fail within the first 18 months."**

*"Five Reasons 8 Out Of 10 Businesses Fail," Eric T. Wagner, Forbes*

Well, here is the reality of the situation, my friend. You must sit down and make detailed revenue goals based upon reality if you are going to be able to manage a team, manage your emotions, manage your bank account, and manage the relationships with investors (should you ever want to have them).

"When you do hard things, life gets easier."

**LEE COCKERELL**
*Thrive15.com Partner / Mentor and the former Executive Vice President of Walt Disney World Resorts who once managed 40,000 cast members*

# Action Items:

1. Buy a White Board.

2. Create a Linear Workflow.

3. Put Your Goals on Your White Board.

4. Write Down the Number of Sales Per Day You Need to Achieve Your Financial Goals.

5. Write Down the Number of No's You Need Per Day to Achieve Your Goals.

RUSH TO REVENUE
Money Cures All Problems

## Story Time: Math Has to Work for Bakeries Too

This reminds me of a client that we worked with years ago. After looking at her numbers it became apparent that based upon her baking capacity and her current pricing that it was impossible for her to ever make more than $40,000 per year. However, once we knew the numbers and knew that denial and blaming weren't viable solutions, we went ahead and raised her prices almost 50 cents per cookie. Because raising her cookie prices by 50 cents did not increase her rent, her payroll, or anything other than her top-line revenue. She was able to increase her income to be able to reach the financial freedom that she was looking for and she only irritated about 5% of her customers in the process.

 ## Story Time: Dog Training on Steroids

After just one month of diligently implementing the 3-legged marketing stool (Search Engine Optimization, Targeting ads on Facebook, and Retargeting ads on Google), the execution of sales scripting, and using a no-brainer offer to close deals, a dog trainer that we worked with got to a place where they were bringing in $2,200 of sales for every $71 they were spending on ads. This company now sees their growth potential and is currently looking for real estate to expand their business.

# EMOTIONAL ROLLER COASTER CHECK

Don't freak out if your revenue goals turn out to not be accurate years, months, or weeks later. As an entrepreneur, you must absolutely be sold out to the rhythm of: DEFINE, ACT, MEASURE, REFINE. You must accept that you can't steer a parked bus. You must keep moving.

1. Define what you think is going to work with your coach.

2. Act after you have gathered all of the facts.

3. Measure the results of the action steps that you have taken without bias.

4. Refine the actions you are taking until you begin to produce the results you are looking for.

DON'T STOP. KEEP MOVING THROUGH THE FOG UNTIL YOU SEE THE LIGHT.

"Success seems to be connected with action. Successful people keep moving. They make mistakes, but they don't quit."

**CONRAD HILTON**
*An American entrepreneur who failed at his attempt to start and grow a successful bank, but later became a successful hotelier and the founder of the Hilton Hotels chain*

RUSH TO REVENUE
Money Cures All Problems

PLOT YOUR COURSE OR YOU WILL
NEVER GET THERE

  **Story Time: Dog Training on Steroids**

One of the cosmetic surgery centers that we've worked with for years was owned by a man who was a skilled surgeon but who had never invested the time to figure out his revenue goals. After spending just one hour with the man, it was determined that certain procedures don't produce much revenue and thus, they really shouldn't be offered unless they were sold in conjunction with the higher revenue producing services. Thus, we started offering Botox as a loss-leader (a deeply discounted item to get people into the door) and aggressively started up-selling the other procedures. Because we invested the time to know how many customers he had to see per week just to break-even, a renewed hustle and sense of urgency began to be seen in both the doctor and the staff. Pretty soon, we took the business to a place where the doctor was able to break-even within the first week of each month. Over time, we cut out the non-effective advertisement that he was doing (billboards and advertising in a magazine that was generating no business) and took the business to a place where he typically now breaks-even on the first day of the month.

# REAL THRIVERS LIKE YOU

"Thanks for all your help last year; we've done a lot of work, reading and investing and the results are truly amazing. Our best staff ever, continuous increases, and overall happiness like never before (and yes more profitable than we've been in years, and while in a down economy)! I feel like we now have entirely new understanding on the importance of culture in the workplace. Do you have any more books you could recommend?! Thanks again Clay!"

*Dave Bauer | www.mymaytagstore.com*

WHAT ARE YOU TRYING TO FIT IN YOUR INCOME BOX?

Chaymations

# REAL THRIVERS LIKE YOU

Barbeescookies.com has been able to quadruple the size of her business in less than 3 years. DelrichtResearch.com has been able to nearly triple their online sales in less than 9 months.

RUSH TO REVENUE
Money Cures All Problems

★ ★ ★ ★ ★
# REAL THRIVERS LIKE YOU

PeakMedicalTech.com has been able to produce over $65,000 of profit in a single month in less than 8 months in the program.

## THE NUMBERS YOU NEED TO KNOW

Determine how much money your business needs to produce per year to fund the pursuit of your F6 Goals (faith, family, friendship, fitness, finance, and fun):

_____

Determine how much money your business needs to produce per month to fund the pursuit of your F6 Goals (faith, family, friendship, fitness, finance, and fun):

_____

### Break Even Formula:
Fixed Costs / Sales Price – Variable Costs = Break Even Point

Determine how much money your business needs to produce per week to fund the pursuit of your F6 Goals (faith, family, friendship, fitness, finance, and fun):

_____

RUSH TO REVENUE
Money Cures All Problems

"SOME PEOPLE DIE AT 25 AND AREN'T BURIED UNTIL 75."
- BENJAMIN FRANKLIN
FOUNDING FATHER OF THE USA

66 .............................................................

"It's not the best-written books that get talked about. It's the best-selling books that we talk about."

**CLAY TIBERIUS CLARK**

66 .............................................................

"Simplicity is the ultimate sophistication."

**STEVE JOBS**
*Co-founder of Apple and the former CEO of PIXAR*

# WARNING!

Do not just create a job, focus on creating a business that has the capacity to provide you with both time and financial freedom.

"What gets scheduled gets done."

**LEE COCKERELL**
*Former Executive Vice President of Walt Disney World Resorts who once managed over 40,000 employees and Thrive15 partner.*

# DESIGN THE LIFE YOU WANT:

| 01 JANUARY | | | | | | 2018 |
|---|---|---|---|---|---|---|
| SUN | MON | TUE | WED | THU | FRI | SAT |
| 31 | 1 | 2 | 3 | 4 | 5 | 6 |
| 7 | 8 | 9 | 10 | 11 | 12 | 13 |
| 14 | 15 | 16 | 17 | 18 | 19 | 20 |
| 21 | 22 | 23 | 24 | 25 | 26 | 27 |
| 28 | 29 | 30 | 31 | 1 | 2 | 3 |
| 4 | 5 | 6 | 7 | 8 | 9 | 10 |

| 01 JANUARY 2018 | 02 FEBRUARY 2018 | 03 MARCH 2018 |
|---|---|---|
| 04 APRIL 2018 | 05 MAY 2018 | 06 JUNE 2018 |
| 07 JULY 2018 | 08 AUGUST 2018 | 09 SEPTEMBER 2018 |
| 10 OCTOBER 2018 | 11 NOVEMBER 2018 | 12 DECEMBER 2018 |

RUSH TO REVENUE
Money Cures All Problems

**CHAPTER 4**

# STEP 2

## ESTABLISH THE NUMBER OF CUSTOMERS NEEDED TO BREAK EVEN AND ACHIEVE FINANCIAL FREEDOM

"Vision without execution is hallucination."

**THOMAS EDISON**
*The man credited as being the founder of GE, and the inventor of the first modern light bulb, recorded sound and recorded audio*

## MYSTIC STATISTIC

**Most businesses don't know the number of customers they need to break even. "4 out of 100 businesses survive past the 10 year mark."**

*"Why 96 Percent of Businesses Fail Within 10 Years," Bill Carmody, Inc Magazine*

## FUN FACT

Thomas Edison holds 1,093 U.S. patent to his name.

## Southwest Airlines Planes Must Be 74.4% Full to Break Even

"Airlines typically have thin profit margins and must have relatively high load factors to stay profitable. In 2014, Southwest Airlines had a break-even load factor of 74.4%. This was lower than most other U.S. major airlines. JetBlue and Delta also had positive load factors, while American and United had non-beneficial load factors. Basically, a Southwest Airlines plane has to be at 74.4% full just to break-even. Around 75% of airline revenue is generated from passengers, with approximately 15% of the remaining revenue from air freight delivery and the remainder from other transport. Passenger earnings are largely generated from domestic travel, so load factor is perhaps particularly relevant on domestic flights. Almost a third of airline fixed costs are associated with flying operations. Another 13% of costs are due to aircraft maintenance, 13% is spent on advertising, 16% on services at the airport gates, 9% on in-flight services, and the rest on other expenses. Significant labor costs are common and account for 75% of an airline's controllable expense."

**INVESTOPEDIA**
*http://www.investopedia.com/ask/answers/041515/how-can-i-use-load-factor-indicator-profitability-airline-industry.asp*

### A Business Doesn't Fail In One Day → They Drift Toward Failure

Years ago, I worked with a bakery that sold wedding cakes and cupcakes. Upon examination of their business numbers, it was determined that with their current business model their profits were so low per item and that they could never produce a profit.

Years ago, we were hired by a franchisee. After helping them to DEEP DIVE into their numbers, we determined that it was not mathematically possible for them to ever generate a profit with the way they were staffing the business. The payroll had to be radically cut, the hours of operation had to be adjusted, and certain items had to stop being offered on the menu and this is not uncommon.

## SUPER PLAYS

Determine how much money your business needs to produce
per year **just to break even:**

_____

### Break Even Formula:
Fixed Costs / Sales Price – Variable Costs = Break Even Point

Determine how much money your business needs to produce
per month **just to break even:**

_____

Determine how much money your business needs to produce
per week **just to break even:**

_____

# NOTES

_____
_____
_____
_____
_____
_____
_____
_____
_____
_____
_____
_____
_____
_____
_____
_____
_____
_____
_____
_____
_____
_____
_____
_____
_____
_____
_____
_____

CHAPTER 5

# STEP 3

## ESTABLISH THE NUMBER OF HOURS YOU ARE WILLING TO WORK ON YOUR BUSINESS

Thomas Edison and his team worked tirelessly on 10,000 failed experiments before successfully creating the world's first practical light bulb.

RUSH TO REVENUE
Money Cures
All Problems

# REAL THRIVERS LIKE YOU

"You certainly were the on-site leader that we needed for this calling campaign. By watching you work with these students and seeing the result, I became reassured that hiring you to do exactly what you did was the right thing to do. Your team brought in over $120K in gifts and pledges, which may be an all-time ORU phonathon record! But I'll have more for you later. I smile to think how funny you were and what a GREAT job you did for us. Again, thanks for everything....and don't drink too much Red Bull!"

*Jesse D. Pisors, B.A. (1996) M.A. (2005)*
*Director of Alumni & Ministerial Relations and Annual Fund*
*Oral Roberts University*

"We often miss opportunity because it's dressed in overalls and looks like hard work."

**THOMAS EDISON**
*Inventor of the modern light bulb, recorded sound and recorded audio*

"Rarely do we find men who willingly engage in hard, solid thinking. There is an almost universal quest for easy answers and half-baked solutions."

**MARTIN LUTHER KING JR.**
*Minister and leader of the Civil Rights Movement*

# How Many Hours Per Week Have You Scheduled to Work On Your Business _____?

You have to be realistic here. Often times we see clients who agree to do things that are not even humanly possible based upon the other obligations they have already signed up for, such as coaching their kids sports teams or planning a wedding. Don't agree to something you can't fulfill and then be frustrated that it isn't happening. If adding additional work time to your schedule, where will this time come from? Family time? Sleep? Will this work for your life? Make sure you are able to be faithful to your other responsibilities.

 ### Story Time: The Elephant In The Room is that Most People Are Unwilling to Work 6 Days Per Week

As an example, I know that when I started the Elephant In The Room Men's Grooming Lounge, I worked 6 days per week doing whatever needed to be done. I refused to work on Sundays. However, today I personally only really work approximately 2 to 3 hours per week in the business. My job is now focused on holding people accountable for the execution of their key performance indicators and for enhancing our repeatable systems. It's super important to be realistic about how much time you are willing to work on your business so that you can block off that time and not commit to doing more action items than you can possibly knock out.

"In all labor there is profit, but mere talk leads only to poverty."

**PROVERBS 14:23**

★ ★ ★ ★ ★

# REAL THRIVERS LIKE YOU

"We have been able to increase our overall sales by nearly 50% as a result of working with Clay for the past 18 months."

*Taylor Hall*
*(General Manager of the Tulsa Oilers Professional Hockey Team.)*

 ## Story Time: Schedule Time for Your Family

Nearly 15 years ago, I used to have a major client who would come to our weekly meetings with the goal of getting everything done and then ending the meetings as soon as possible. He owned a massively successful company and we always knocked out everything on his agenda, but I was curious about why he always made sure to end our 1-hour meetings within 20 to 30 minutes. One day, I asked him what his schedule looked like after our weekly meeting. His response was EPIC and I certainly did not expect it. He said (and I'm paraphrasing), "Clay, I always have my Friday chiropractic adjustment and massage booked 45 minutes after this meeting so that I won't miss my tee time at the Golf Course. You know Fridays are date night with my wife so I have to try to squeeze it all in." The profundity of this concept blew my mind. This man was literally scheduling in time for his wife, his pleasure, his hobbies, and the pursuit of his goals just like everybody schedules time for work.

"Time management is not about managing your time, it's about keeping your whole life under control. Plan the life you want or live the life you don't want."

**LEE COCKERELL**
*Our Thrive15.com Partner and the guy that used to manage over 40,000 employees as the former head of Walt Disney World Resort*

RUSH TO REVENUE
Money Cures All Problems

# DESIGN THE LIFE YOU WANT

Today, take out your calendar and write into your schedule the hours that you are willing to work on the various F6 aspects of your life (as an example, I will not work on Sundays, unless it is a super rare occasion).

Write out the boundaries with your time and schedule that you are not willing to cross. As an example, when I first started my businesses, I was willing to work every hour of every day Monday through Sunday. Now, I will not meet people for lunch, attend work related parties, go out to dinner with clients, or ever leave my office during the workday. I turn my phone off every weekend, all weekend and I don't return calls of any kind that relate to work on the weekends.

Create one master calender that includes your work life & personal life...in 1 hour time blocks.

Boundary 1: _____

Boundary 2: _____

Boundary 3: _____

Boundary 4: _____

Boundary 5: _____

★ ★ ★ ★ ★

# REAL THRIVERS LIKE YOU

It took Thrive15.com mentor and best selling author nearly 3 years to close his first deal as he introduced the Stairmaster to the marketplace.

*Clifton Taulbert*

RUSH TO REVENUE
Money Cures All Problems

## OPTIMIZE YOUR LIFESTYLE

Write Down a List of the Activities That You Are Going to Stop Doing:

_____

_____

_____

_____

_____

## OPTIMIZE THE PEOPLE IN YOUR LIFE

Write Down a List of the People You Will No Longer Spend Time With:

_____

_____

_____

_____

_____

# CHAPTER 6

# STEP 4

## DETERMINE YOUR UNIQUE VALUE PROPOSITION

## EXAMPLES

- Whole Foods (chalk menus, employees w/ dreadlocks)

- Disney (music, clean, customer service)

- Starbucks (smells good, speed)

- Apple Store (customer service, modern, innovative)

- In & Out (great food, simple menu, fast)

- Chick-Fil-A (my pleasure, service)

- Software

- Site / Smells

- Health Plans

## THE WOW FACTOR

## "You must wow customers to increase net promoter score."

**CLAY CLARK**
*Former U.S. SBA Entrepreneur of the year and Captain Obvious*

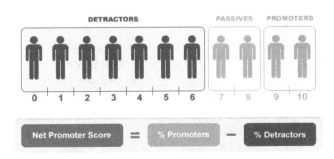

"In a crowded marketplace fitting in is failing...Not standing out is the same as being invisible. Boring is invisible. Remarkable people and products get talked about."

**SETH GODIN**
*Best-selling author and marketing guru who sold his business Yoyodyne to Yahoo! For $30 million*

In order to build a successful business, you must find a way to stand-out from your competition in a compelling, repeatable, and memorable way that truly connects with your ideal and likely buyers. You can't just say, "customer service" is what sets us apart. You can't just say, "professionalism" is what sets us apart. You can't say, "our history of excellence" is what sets us apart. You must truly set yourself apart in a way that is compelling, repeatable, and memorable to your ideal and likely buyers.

## Starbucks

The decor and atmosphere is designed to create what the CEO Howard Schultz calls the "third place." They have baristas instead of coffee people. They use unique words to describe their sizes. Their artwork is unique. Their overhead music is intentional. Their sight, build-out, decor, sounds, smells, ambiance, atmosphere, and nomenclature truly set them apart in addition to their great customer service.

## Tom's Shoes

Every time you and I buy a pair of shoes, they give a pair to a person in need. This giveback program has provided the founder, Blake Mycoskie, with a sustainable way to giveback to those in need and it generates sustainably high amounts of word of mouth for his business.

"Giving feels good, but it's also good for the bottom line. Charity is a viable growth strategy for a lot of companies. Our customers get excited to be a part of what we're doing. If you ask anyone wearing Toms how they first heard about us, most won't mention an advertisement; they'll say a friend told them our story."

**BLAKE MYCOSKIE**
*Founder of Toms Shoes*

## Doctor Robert H. Zoellner and Associates

Doctor Robert H. Zoellner and Associates is now one of the most successful eye-wear and optometry clinics in Oklahoma and that's because of his pigheaded discipline when it comes to running his radio commercials. Most people know about this business. Dr. Zoellner is always running commercials promoting his $99.00 get one pair of stylish eye glasses and an exam. He's been running that same promotion for nearly 25 years and although only 7% of his customers choose to take advantage of that special, everyone in town knows about him because of his on-going commercials.

## Elephant In The Room

Elephant In The Room is a high-end men's grooming lounge that is basically like a high-end country club for hair. The name is memorable and the decor is a mix of modern rustic buildout historic barnwood, Edison bulbs, and old school over-sized barber chairs. We offer every customer a free beverage, a hot towel treatment, and a tailored haircut experience. Also, the first time someone comes in for their haircut, it's always just $1.00, which we can afford because of our membership model.

Don't be a DMV ---> **Compare a Purple Cow Business to a Brown Cow Business**

110

> "You're either a Purple Cow or you're not. You're either remarkable or invisible. Make your choice."

**SETH GODIN**
*Best-selling author of Purple Cow, marketing guru, and the man who sold a company he started called At Yoyodyne. Godin published Permission Marketing: Turning strangers into friends and friends into customers. In 1998, he sold his marketing firm Yoyodyne to Yahoo! for about $30 million*

"IN A CROWDED MARKETPLACE, FITTING IN IS FAILING. IN A BUSY MARKETPLACE, NOT STANDING OUT IS THE SAME AS BEING INVISIBLE."
- SETH GODIN
BEST-SELLING AUTHOR OF "PURPLE COW"

## Why Aren't People Buying?

No Need
No Time (Too Busy)
No Money
No Time Pressure

No Video Reviews
No Google Reviews
No Amazon Reviews
No Faith in Your Branding

## FUN FACT

From my life experience approximately 15% of customers will take advantage of you.

*Clay Clark*

RUSH TO REVENUE
Money Cures All Problems

# CREATE YOUR NO BRAINER TODAY

---

Determine a sustainable giveback program (like Toms Shoes, Warby Parker, Starbucks, etc.).

---

Create a NO-BRAINER OFFER that your competition isn't willing to do (an offer so good that your ideal and likely buyers almost can't say no).

Examples of NO-BRAINER OFFERS:

1. Buy One Get One Free

2. $1.00 First Purchase

3. Freemium

4. Try It Before You Buy It

5. Money Back Guarantee

6. Samples

7. Deep Discounts

8. Endorsement from a World-Class Celebrity (George Foreman endorsed the Lean Mean Fat-Reducing Grilling Machine and sold over 100 million units. His endorsement deal involved him getting paid a percentage of the sales instead of amount of money up upfront).

## Ample Examples:

**Elephant In The Room** – $1.00 first haircut

**Dr. Robert Zoellner and Associates** – $99 first eye exam and pair of stylish glasses

**Tylenol** – Maximum Strength

Create a smell that wows your customers when they first interact with your brand (fresh cookies, burning pinion wood, smoked barbecue, etc.)

Create a music playlist that will wow your ideal and likely buyers.

Create an inbound phone script that will wow your ideal and likely buyers.

Create an outbound sales script that will wow your ideal and likely buyers.

Create a mass text campaign (Pizza Hut consistently will send out weekly texts to stay top in your mind)

Create a mass email campaign (Numerous large companies will use AWeber or Constant Contact)

Create a mass voicemail campaign (this is where you can leave hundreds of messages to people using a program called Slybroadcast)

Create employee uniforms that will wow your customers / guests (the bellman at Trump hotels are legendary, Michael Jackson's white glove was memorable, the staff at the Disney Store in the mall all wear Disney themed clothing, the uniforms of Sonic employees are memorable to many).

Provide generous samples and product demonstrations that showcase what your business can do.

RUSH TO REVENUE
Money Cures All Problems

Develop a memorable experience unlike anybody else. (flying rolls, donut assembly line, etc.)

Create a customer interaction that can't be forgotten (The Build-A-Bear store has found a way to actually charge us for allowing our own kids to make their own stuffed animals, the decor in the Rainforest Cafe is memorable, etc.)

Create a distinctive build-out in terms of your physical office space (Zappos keeps things interesting, Starbucks is very intentional, the Warren Theatres are gorgeous, the Elephant In The Room brings manly modern rustic to every store, Doctor Robert Zoellner and Associates optometry clinics make you feel like you are in a mall and not at an optometrist's office, etc.)

Create business cards that wow (in the shape of unique things related to the products and services you offer).

Offer samples to your customers (many high-end grocery stores have found a way to compete with the big box stores by offering an abundant amount of food samples to shoppers).

Build a massive or iconic landmark in front of your business or building.

| | BUYING FACTOR A | BUYING FACTOR B | BUYING FACTOR C | |
|---|---|---|---|---|
| YOUR COMPANY | | | | |
| COMPETITOR A | | | | |
| COMPETITOR B | | | | |
| COMPETITOR C | | | | |

RUSH TO REVENUE
Money Cures All Problems

# THE PURPLE COW CHECKLIST

1. What is your Unique Service Offering?
   (Elephant in the Room Experience)

2. What is your Unique Product Offering?
   (DrZoellner.com)

3. Describe your Unique Decor:
   (Rainforest Cafe, Krispy Kreme)

4. Describe your Unique Music / Ambiance:
   (Victoria Secret, Howl at the Moon, H&M)

5. Describe your Unique Experience:
   (Wholefoods, Samples Everywhere)

6. Describe your Unique Smell:
   (Starbucks, Auntie Ann's Pretzels, Godiva)

7. Describe your Unique Branding
   (Chick-Fil-A, Purple Cow, Harley, Starbucks)

8. Give Back:
   (Tom's Shoes: Buy a pair, give a pair!)

9. Deep Empathy:
   (What does our ideal and likely buyer want: West Jet Christmas Miracle)

10. Experience:
    (Early Southwest Airlines Uniforms, Dick's Last Resort & Bar, Howling at the Moon)

RUSH TO
REVENUE
Money Cures
All Problems

**CHAPTER 7**

# STEP 5

## IMPROVE BRANDING

"People do judge pieces of jewelry by the packaging, books by their covers, and businesses based upon their branding."

**CLAY CLARK**
*Former SBA Entrepreneur of the Year*

116

"If you give someone a present, and you give it to them in a Tiffany box, it's likely that they'll believe that the gift has higher perceived value than if you gave it to them in no box or a box of less prestige. That's not because the receiver of the gift is a fool. But instead, because we live in a culture in which we gift wrap everything — our politicians, our corporate heads, our movie and TV stars, and even our toilet paper."

**MICHAEL LEVINE**
*Thrive15.com mentor and the man who has been the PR consultant for Michael Jackson, Prince, Nike, Pizza Hut, Nancy Kerrigan, and many other celebrities and large brands*

**Ample Example**

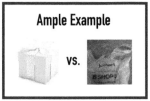

As an example, Steve Jobs wanted to make packaging and boxes that were such high-quality that people would keep them and not know what to do with them after they purchased a computer, iPad, or any Apple product.

As an example, Doctor Zoellner and his team at the auto auction (Z66AA.com) are constantly sprucing up the look of everything so that people have a great first impression of the business. In fact, he involves the letter Z in every business that he owns because it's gotten to the point where pretty much everybody in Tulsa knows his name which makes people feel more comfortable when using a business that has his familiar branding.

**Ample Example**

"We made buttons on the screen look so good you'll want to lick them."

**STEVE JOBS**
*(Co-founder of Apple, and former CEO of Pixar)*

RUSH TO REVENUE
Money Cures All Problems

## Bad Looking Websites Hurt Your Wallet:

As an example, years ago, I worked with a high-end photographer in Dallas who may have had the world's worst website and so very few brides were willing to work with him because the elephant in the room was that if his website looked so bad, his wedding photos were probably bad too. I was able to help him dramatically improve the brand of his company and eventually bought the guy out of the company that is now called EpicPhotos.com.

## From a Fireworks Stand to a National Power House:

As an example, OxiFresh.com, who we've worked with, is now the world's greenest carpet cleaner with over 300 functioning franchises around the world. When I first met Jonathan, he was a college student who owned a firework stand. However, over time Jonathan built a massively successful franchise called OxiFresh.com. The key to selling franchises is having a great product, turn-key marketing, and world-class large-company-looking branding. You essentially have to look big before you are.

"Marketing is a contest for people's attention."

**SETH GODIN**
*(The founder of Yoyodyne, which he sold to Yahoo for $30 million before becoming a best-selling author and branding / marketing expert)*

### Deep Thoughts

"If you don't learn to sell while you're alive, eventually you'll have to dumpster dive."

**CLAY CLARK**
*A man who continues to stay married to the same woman*

RUSH TO REVENUE
Money Cures All Problems

# SUPER MOVES FOR ENHANCING YOUR BRANDING

1. Create a website that is better than your competition.

2. Create a logo that is better than your competition.

3. Create a one sheet that clearly shows the value between you and the competition.

4. Create print materials that are better than your competition.

5. Create a marketing video that succinctly explains what problems you solve, who you are, and why people should buy from you.

6. Create signage that will wow your ideal and likely buyers.

7. Make sure that everything that your customers see or experience is first-class and intentional.

8. Create Google My Business account: business.google.com.

9. Get Google reviews.

10. Gather testimonial videos from your happy clients.

11. Have your team wear memorable uniforms.

12. Create a story video.

# EXAMPLES OF WORLD'S BEST LOGOS

## Deep Thoughts

"After working with many businesses. When people can't sell a lot they end up writing poetry, quoting Bob Dylan, living in a park in downtown Denver and smoking pot."

**CLAY CLARK**
*A man-bear-pig who tricked a queen into marrying him.*

## Deep Thoughts:

"I have worked with many businesses who get stuck in the 'logo stage' of business. If you get stuck on the 'logo stage', your company will never grow and you will start living in a van down by the river."

**ROBERT REDMOND**
*Business Coach, ThriveTime Show, & RGC*

**Oklahoma District Office**
301 NW 6ᵗʰ Street, Suite 116  Oklahoma City, OK  73102   405/609-8000   (fax) 405/609-8990

February 21, 2007

Mr. Clayton Thomas Clark
DJ Connection Tulsa, Inc.
8900 South Lynn Lane Road
Broken Arrow, Oklahoma 74102

Dear Mr. Clark:

Congratulations!  You have been selected as the **2007 Oklahoma SBA Young Entrepreneur of the Year**.  On behalf of the U.S. Small Business Administration (SBA), I wish to express our appreciation for your support of small business and for your contributions to the economy of this State.

In recognition of your achievement, **an awards luncheon will be held Tuesday, May 22, 2007** at Rose State College in Midwest City, Okla. The luncheon is sponsored by the Oklahoma Small Business Development Center. Two complimentary luncheon tickets have been reserved for you and one guest.

Arrangements for the luncheon are still being finalized.  You will be notified of the details as soon as they become available. You are encouraged to bring family, friends, and business associates.  Upon presentation of your award, you will have the opportunity to make acceptance comments.

Also, for our awards brochure, please email an electronic photo of yourself to darla.booker@sba.gov by Friday, March 16.

Again, congratulations on your outstanding accomplishment.

Sincerely,

Dorothy (Dottie) A. Overal
Oklahoma District Director

"When you implement a proven system, you will achieve predictable results."

**CLAY CLARK**
*Founder of ThriveTimeShow.com, former U.S. SBA Entrepreneur of the Year, host of the ThriveTime Show, and America's #1 Business Coach*

**CHAPTER 8**

# STEP 6

## CREATE A 3-LEGGED MARKETING STOOL

- Dream 100
- Adwords
- Retargeting Ads
- Q&A
- How to get Google Reviews
- Determine Where Your Ideal & Likely Buyers Are

"Inaction is the giant. Action is the sword. Inspiration is the reward."

**CLAY CLARK**
*(Former U.S. SBA Entrepreneur of the year and the son of the late great Thom Clark.)*

"Diligence is the consistant application of effort."

**CLAY CLARK**
*(A Recovering DJ / Man-bear-pig)*

"The missing ingredient for nearly all of the 1,000-plus clients I have worked with directly to improve their businesses is pigheaded discipline and determination. We all get good ideas at seminars and from books, radio talk shows and business-building gurus. The problem is that most companies do not know how to identify and adapt the best ideas to their businesses. Implementation, not ideas, is the key to real success."

**CHET HOLMES**
*Former business partner of billionaire Charlie Munger and the best-selling author of The Ultimate Sales Machine*

Claymations

"I'M A GREAT BELIEVER IN LUCK, AND I FIND THE HARDER I WORK, THE MORE I HAVE OF IT."
- THOMAS JEFFERSON
3RD PRESIDENT OF THE USA

## The Power of the Three-Legged Marketing Stool:

As an example, Elephant In The Room acquires customers in only three repeatable systems that we execute diligently every day. 1st - We put out $1.00 first haircut signs in front of each location. 2nd - We write 5 articles every day for the website which makes us top in Google. 3rd - We do mailers and online ads that show up in your mailbox, on Facebook, and other websites that people visit. It's not about having a thousand marketing systems, it's about executing a limited number of turn-key systems that work over and over again.

"Simple can be harder than complex: You have to work hard to get your thinking clean to make it simple. But it's worth it in the end because once you get there, you can move mountains."

**STEVE JOBS**
*Co-founder of Apple and the former CEO of PIXAR*

"Keep your sales pipeline full by prospecting continuously. Always have more people to see than you have time to see them."

**BRIAN TRACY**
*Best-selling author and renowned sales trainer*

"Commit to your long-term success and forget about your short-term stress."

**CLAY CLARK**
*(A man who tricked his wife into marrying him.)*

# DESCRIBE YOUR IDEAL AND LIKELY BUYER

**Write down a description of who your ideal and likely buyers are:**

1. Men or Women or Both?

2. Average Age?

3. Average Income Level?

4. Geographical Location?

5. Places They Go?

6. Schools Their Kids Attend?

7. Search Terms They Type Into Search Engines?

8. Shared Fears?

9. Shared Goals?

10. Shared Hobbies and Interests?

11. Shared Problems?

12. Sports Their Kids Play?

13. Stores They Shop At?

14. Types of Cars They Drive?

15. Proven Ad, Landing Page, Set Budget

From the list below, circle which marketing vehicles that you think are most likely to carry your marketing message effectively to your ideal and likely buyers:

Adwords

Amazon.com

Automobile Wraps

Billboard Advertising

Blog Based Advertising

Business Development / Partnership Deals

Buying Your Competition / Mergers and Acquisition

Celebrity Endorsement

Cold Call Marketing

Door to Door Sales

Dream 100

Email Marketing

Facebook Advertising

Flyers

Google Maps

Google Reviews

Google Shopping

Magazine Advertising

Mall / Shopping Center Traffic

Mass Mailers

Mass Texting (Twilio)

Mass Voicemails (Slybroadcast)

Mass Emails (AWeber, Constant Contact)

Networking Intentionally (Set number of meetings per month and specific organizations)

Newspaper Advertising

Outdoor Signage

Pandora.com Radio Advertising

Pay Per Click - Search Engine Marketing / Advertising

Pop-Up Shop

Public Relations
- Celebrity Tie-In Strategy
- Expert Strategy
- Giveback Strategy
- National News Tie-In Strategy
- Shock and Awe Strategy

Radio Advertising

Referral Based Advertising

Retargeting Online ads (See SEO Conversion checklist)

Search Engine Optimization (See next pages for details)

Sign-Based Marketing

Sign-Flipper Marketing

Social Media Advertising

Speech Based Marketing

Spotify Advertising

Targeted Online ads

Television Advertising

Text Marketing

Trade Show Advertising

Valpak Advertising

Yelp Reviews

YouTube Advertising

### Bias Alert... But Still True

ThriveTime Show sponsors make more money than they spend on advertising.

## BUSINESS TO BUSINESS MARKETING CHECKLIST

### DREAM 100
1. Mailer
2. Business Card
3. Script
4. Record Calls
5. Drop off Items

### REPUTATION MANAGEMENT
1. Google Reviews
2. Testimonial Videos

### RETARGETING ADS

### TRADESHOW MANAGEMENT
1. Purple Cow
2. Booth Design
3. Sign-Up Registration / Giveaway / Chance to Win
4. Lead Sheets
5. Team Training
6. One Sheet

## ADWORDS TEMPLATE

1.  Set your budget

2.  Determine 10 Keywords

3.  Geographical Location That You Are Targeting

4.  The Actual Ad:
    What do you want the offer to say in the google listing

5.  Where is it going?

## FACEBOOK ADS

1.  Demographics (Income Level, Age, Gender, Geographic location)

2.  Set Budget (Minimum $5 per day)

3.  Create a landing page

4.  Never stop running ads

    •   Facebook makes you get ads approved before launched

    •   Facebook rewards people who are consistent

    •   Facebook has an anti-scam rule that flags users who launches ads then shut them down

    •   You lose credibility if you launch ads, then don't see them anymore - people will trust an ad after they see it more often

"Call Them Until they Cry, Buy, or Die!"

**CLAY CLARK**
*The guy who follows the above mantra religiously, and has seen massive success from following said mantra.*

# WUPHF! YOUR LEADS

1. Leave mass voicemails using slybroadcast.com

2. Send mass texts using Twilio.com

3. Send mass e-mails (aWeber, MailChimp)

4. Call all leads until they cry, buy, or die

"Some will. Some won't. Who Cares!? LET'S GO!"

**CLAY CLARK**

*The humanoid who puts more time and energy into caring about his wife, 5 kids, and silky chickens than what a complete stranger said on the phone the other day.*

RUSH TO REVENUE
Money Cures All Problems

<header class="chapter-title">

<p>CHAPTER 2</p>

<h1>

# ULTIMATE SEARCH ENGINE DOMINATION CHECKLIST

</h1>

</header>

```
<style>
    #page-background{
        background-color: #DB4437;
    }
        .chapter-title p{
            text-transform: uppercase;
            color: white;
            font-family: 'Proxima Nova';
            font-weight: 600;
        }

        .chapter-title h1{
            text-transform: uppercase;
            color: white;
            font-family: 'Proxima Nova';
            font-weight: 900;
        }
</style>
```

RUSH TO REVENUE
Money Cures All Problems

In order for you to achieve total SEARCH ENGINE DOMINATION and DRAMATICALLY increase your level of COMPENSATION you must simply check off and complete all of the checklist items on this website evaluation. We humbly refer to this checklist as "The Ultimate Search Engine Domination Checklist."

# The Ultimate Search Engine DOMINATION Checklist

(and Website Evaluation):

_____ **Host your website with a reliable hosting service.** If your website is hosted with an unreliable hosting service you will rank lower in the search engines. We recommend using GoDaddy.com. Don't host your website with some local, janky hosting provider who lives with his mom in the basement.

_____ **Host your website with the fastest package that you can afford.** Google REALLY CARES about how long it takes for your website to load. Why? Because people get impatient and will quickly move on to another website if your website takes too long to load. On January 17th of 2018, Google formally announced the "Speed Update." Google's plan called for them to slowly roll out the new search engine ranking criteria to give web-developers plenty of time to make their websites load much, much faster. To test the speed of your website visit: https://developers.google.com/speed/pagespeed/insights/ To read more about Google's new speed requirements visit: https://www.forbes.com/sites/jaysondemers/2018/01/29/will-googles-new-page-speed-criteria-affect-your-site/#396634ed6a8f

_____ **Build your website on the WordPress platform**. "WordPress offers the best out-of-the-box search engine optimization imaginable." - Tim Ferriss (Best-selling author of *The 4-Hour Work Week*, *The 4-Hour Body*, *The 4-Hour Chef*, *Tools of Titans*, and *Tribe of Mentors*. He is also an early stage investor in Facebook, Twitter, Evernote, Uber, etc.)

Don't use any other website building platform than WordPress. If you hire coders to custom build your website on PHP or .NET you will end up hating your life as a result of having a website that nobody can update other than the entitled, nefarious employees who now have the ability to hold you hostage. Trust us here. We have personally coached hundreds of clients and every time our coaching clients have a custom built website the business owner at some point has been held hostage by the employee who is the only person who knows how to update the custom built, non-search engine friendly, and ridiculously complicated website. Building your website on WordPress puts the power back in your hands as a business owner because you can update the website yourself if you have to.

## PRO TIP: USE WORDPRESS.ORG NOT WORDPRESS.COM

*WordPress.org is the open source platform used to power the best SEO compliant websites in the world. WordPress.com is their platform that does not allow for plugins or optimal website optimization.*

*\*Avoid WordPress.com*

 _____ **Build a mobile-friendly website.** What is a mobile friendly website? Check your website's mobile compliance at: https://search.google.com/test/mobile-friendly. If this link changes in the future just search for "Google mobile compliance test" in the Google search engine and you'll find it.

_____ **Install HTTPS encryption onto your website.**
HTTPS encryption stands for Hypertext Transfer Protocol
Secure. What does that mean? HTTPS encryption makes
your website more difficult for bad people to hack, thus
making it tougher for very bad people to crash your
website and to use your website as a way to steal the
personal information of your valuable clients and patrons.
Google ranks websites higher who have invested the
additional money needed to add HTTPS encryption to
their website. How many times would you use Google if
every time their search results sent you to websites that
had been hacked into by cyber criminals and internet
hackers?

 _____**Install the Yoast.com search engine optimization
plugin into your website.** What is Yoast? Yoast SEO is
the best WordPress plugin on the planet when it comes
to search engine optimization. Yoast was built and
designed in a way to make search engine optimization
approachable for everyone, and thus we love Yoast.
Yoast makes it possible for people who are not
complete nerds to proactively manage the search
engine optimization of their website.

 DEFINITION MAGICIAN
**Plugin** - A plugin is a piece of code or software that provides a
variety of functions that you can add to your WordPress website.
Plugins allow you to increase the functional capacity of your website
without having to hire a bunch of nefarious, entitled custom coders
who are typically hard to manage because you do not have any idea
what they are working on or what they are talking about 90% of the
time.

**_____Uniquely optimize every meta title tag on every page of your website.**
The title tag is simply a hypertext markup language (HTML) element on a website that specifies to search engines what a particular web page is all about. "according to SEOMoz, the best practice for the title tag length is to keep titles under 70 characters." An example would be, "Full Package Media | Dallas Real Estate Photography | 972-885-8823"

Full Package Media | Dallas Real Estate Photography | 972-885-8823
https://fullpackagemedia.com/ ▼
Looking for the best in the business when it comes to **Dallas** Real Estate Photography? You need to

 **_____Uniquely optimize every meta description on every page of your website.** The meta description is simply part of the hypertext markup language (HTML) code that provides a brief summary about a web page. Search engines like Google usually show the meta description in search engine results. Don't make your meta descriptions more than 160 characters in length.

An ample example would be, "Looking for the best in the business when it comes to Dallas Real Estate Photography? You need to call Full Package Media today at 972-885-8823."

Looking for the best in the business when it comes to **Dallas** Real Estate Photography? You need to call **Full Package Media** today at 972-885-8823.
Careers · About Us · Contact Us · Client Login

 **_____Uniquely optimize the keywords on every page of your website.** Meta keywords are a very specific kind of meta tag that will show up in the hypertext markup language (HTML) code on web pages and these will tell the search engines what the web page is really all about. An example of specific keyword optimization would be "Berj Najarian." You may be thinking, who is Berj Najarian?

Berj Najarian serves as the New England Patriots Director of Football and the "Chief of Staff" for the legendary Coach Bill Belichick who has won a total of 8 Super Bowl titles since beginning his coaching career in the National Football League. If someone is searching for "Berj Najarian" there is a high probability that they already know who "Berj Najarian" is and if you want to rank high in the search engines when people are searching for "Berj Najarian" you definitely want to make sure that you have declared your meta keyword phrase as "Berj Najarian."

**Quick Note:** If at any point while reading this you are beginning to feel overwhelmed just submit your website for an audit and deep dive evaluation and we'll do the heavy lifting for you. You can submit your website to be audited at: www.ThrivetimeShow.com/Website

_____ **Create 1,000 words of original and relevant text (content) per page on your website.** Are we saying that somebody actually has to write, 1,000 original words of original and relevant text for every page of your website? Yes. Isn't there a hack? NO. Can't there be a better way? No.

Can't you just go out and hire a company out of India to use "spinners" to slightly change existing text for you? NO. Can't you just copy content from another website? NO.

You can spend every minute of every day trying to find some blogger or some website experts out there that will tell you that someone on your team doesn't need to invest the time needed to create 1,000 words of both original and relevant content and you will eventually find them and they will be 100% wrong. However, they will gladly take your money.

Google    berj najarian

All    Images    News    Shopping    Videos    More        Settings    Tools

About 6,450 results (0.38 seconds)

*META TITLE TAG*

Who is Berj Najarian? | Bill Belichick's Secret Weapon | Thrivetimeshow
https://www.thrivetimeshow.com/.../berj-najarian-the-80-20-rule-the-new-england-pat... ▾
★★★★★ Rating: 4.9 - 2,651 reviews
**Berj Najarian** is Bill Belichick's Chief of Staff he's the human on the planet that has spent the most time
with Bill Belichick since he became the New England ...

*PERMALINK*

*META DESCRIPTION*

Who is the mysterious Berj Najarian, Bill Belichick's right-hand man ...
https://www.bostonglobe.com/sports/patriots/2019/01/31/...berj-najarian.../story.html
Jan 31, 2019 - **Najarian** is one of the most powerful figures on the Boston sports landscape, yet most
fans have never heard of him.

Images for berj najarian

→ More images for berj najarian                    Report images

YOU OR A MEMBER OF YOUR TEAM MUST WRITE
1,000 WORDS OF ORIGINAL AND RELEVANT
CONTENT FOR EVERY PAGE OF YOUR WEBSITE.

_____ **Create a Google search engine compliant
.XML sitemap on your website.** What is an .XML
sitemap? XML stands for Extensible Markup Language.
A quality XML sitemap serves as a map of your website
which allows the Google search engine to find all of
the important pages located within your website. As
a website owner unless you hate money, you REALLY
WANT GOOGLE to be able to crawl (find, rank, and
sort) all of the important pages on your website. Yoast.
com has tools that will actually generate Google
compliant .XML sitemaps for you. Don't worry, you can
do this!

**Fun Fact:** *I had to take Algebra 3 times en route
to getting into Oral Roberts University and I was
eventually kicked out of college for writing a
parody about the school's president "ORU Slim
Shady" which you can currently find on YouTube.
If I can learn and master search engine
optimization you can too!*

RUSH TO
REVENUE
Money Cures
All Problems

136

 _____**Create a Google search engine compliant HTML sitemap.** What's an HTML site map? A hypertext markup language sitemap allows the people who visit your website to easily navigate your website. This sitemap should be located at the bottom of your website and should be labeled as a "Sitemap."

Hiding your sitemap for any reason is a bad idea because Google assumes that if you are hiding your sitemap you are probably trying to hide something. Don't change the background of your website to be the same color as your sitemap's font or do anything tricky here. You want to make sure that your website's sitemap can easily be found at the bottom of your website. See the example below:

 _____**Create a clickable phone number.** If you ever want to sell something to humans on the planet Earth you must make your contact information easy to find. Thus you want to make your phone number easily available to find at either the top right or at the bottom of your website. When coaching your web-developer, force them to make your phone number a "click-to-call" phone number so that users on your website who are using a mobile phone (almost everyone) can simply click the number to call you.

In our shameless attempt to make this the BEST, MOST HUMBLE and the MOST ACTIONABLE SEARCH ENGINE OPTIMIZATION book of all time we have provided the following real examples from REAL clients just like you who we have really helped to REALLY increase their REAL sales year after year:

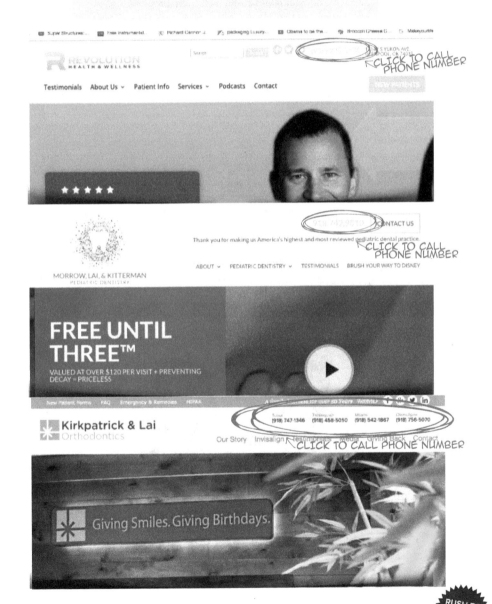

**\_\_\_\_\_Have a Social Proof.** If you don't hate money and you are not a committed socialist, you will want to include some social proof near the top of your website. What is social proof? "Social proof" is a phrase and a term that was original created by the best-selling author Robert Cialdini in his book, **Influence**. The best social proof examples are:

a. Real testimonials from real current and former clients is super powerful.

b. Media features and appearances on credible media sources like Bloomberg, Fox Business, Entrepreneur.com, Fast Company, etc.

c. Proudly showing that you have earned the highest and most reviews in your local business niche.

d. Celebrity endorsements from celebrities that have earned the trust of your ideal and likely buyers.

e. Listed below is an example that will showcase to you what it looks like to use social proof effectively.

**_____Make the logo return to home.** Allow the logo on your website to serve as your "homepage" button. As of 2019, most people assume that if they click your logo they are going to be taken back to the homepage of your website.

 **_____Create original content.** You must create more original and relevant content than anyone else in the world about your specific search engine focus. If you want to come up top in the world for the phrase "organic supplements" you must then create the most original and relevant content on the planet about "organic supplements." If you want to come up top in your city for the phrase "knee pain Tulsa" then you must what? You must create the most original and relevant content on the planet about "knee pain Tulsa."

If you want to come up top in the search engine results for the phrase "America's #1 business coach" then you must create the most original and relevant content on the planet about "America's #1 business coach." Listed below are a few examples of receiving high search rankings due to having the most original, relevant content on the planet about that particular subject.

---

america's #1 business coach    🎤  🔍

All    News    Images    Videos    Maps    More          Settings    Tools

About 5,870,000 results (0.35 seconds)

Business Coach | Bill Belichick's #1 Fan and America's #1 Business ...
https://www.thrivetimeshow.com/the...show/business-coach-management-principles/ ▾
★★★★★ Rating: 99% · 2,651 votes
Bill Belichick's number one fan and **America's #1 business coach** Clay Clark teaches many of the successful management principles that Belichick ...

People also ask

Who is the best business coach in the world?                              ⌄

What should I look for in a business coach?                               ⌄

1.3 mi · 3019 E 101st St · (918) 299-4415 ext. 5384

WEBSITE   DIRECTIONS

### The Little Gym of SE Tulsa
4.7 ★★★★★ (14) · Gymnastics center
3.3 mi · 6556 E 91st St · (918) 492-2626
Open · Closes 7:30PM
🌐 Their website mentions **gymnastics classes**

WEBSITE   DIRECTIONS

### Twist & Shout Tumbling & Cheer
3.5 ★★★★★ (8) · Gym
6.2 mi · 4820 S 83rd E Ave · (918) 622-5867
Closed · Opens 5PM
🌐 Their website mentions **tumbling classes**

WEBSITE   DIRECTIONS

≡  More places

### Tumbling Tulsa | Tulsa Tumbling Lessons | 918-764-8804
https://justicetumblingco.com/ ▾
If you are looking for the best and highest reviewed **tumbling Tulsa** place, you need to call us at Justice
**Tumbling** today and see what makes us better.
Services · About · Schedule · Testimonials

### Tulsa Cheerleading | Tumbling Tulsa | Tulsa Tumbling | 918-986-5785
https://tumblesmart.com/ ▾
**Tulsa's** Most Reviewed **Tumbling** Program. **Tumble** Smart Athletics. Free Evaluation **Lesson**Meet the
Owner. **Tumbling Tulsa** Gymnast Stars. Experience the

Google    tulsa knee pain

*META TITLE TAG*

### Tulsa Knee Pain - Revolution Health Tulsa
https://www.revolutionhealth.org/.../tulsa-knee-pain-revolution-health-is-bring-in-a-re... ▾
Find the best treatment for your **Tulsa knee pain** right here in Tulsa. Find out more about Revolution
Health by calling at 918-935-3636.

*PERMALINK*

*META DESCRIPTION*

### Tulsa knee Pain | Revolution Health Oklahoma
https://www.revolutionhealth.org/.../tulsa-knee-pain-find-the-top-and-quickest-result-f... ▾
The best prolotherapy is right here at Revolution Health for **Tulsa knee pain**.

### Best Prolotherapy Treatments Tulsa | Tulsa Knee Pain
https://www.revolutionhealth.org/.../tulsa-knee-pain-find-the-best-possible-tulsa-knee-... ▾
Best 30 the Best Prolotherapy Treatments for your **tulsa knee Pain**

### Non-invasive remedies relieve knee pain without surgery - Tulsa World
https://www.tulsaworld.com/...knee-pain/.../article_6bdf681d-d017-554c-9ecc-fae529... ▾
Mar 13, 2019 · Dear Doctor K: I have osteoarthritis of the knee. Are there ways to relieve my **knee pain**
without drugs or surgery?

_____**Create a "Testimonials," "Case Studies," or a "Success Stories" portion of your website** if you want to sell something to humans who were not born yesterday. Most shoppers today have become savvy and are aware of the fact that great companies generate great reviews (and occasionally bad ones) and that bad companies chronically generate bad reviews (and occasionally some good ones). Thus, most people will want to actually see testimonials, case studies or success stories from real clients that have actually worked with your company in the past.

In fact, not having testimonials, case studies, and success stories on your website freaks most people out to the point that they won't even call you or fill out your contact form.

How do we know this? Well, for starters, we are humans who happen to be also consumers and Forbes tells us that, "Almost 90% of consumers said they read reviews for local businesses. In other words, if you are not investing efforts into online reputation management, then you are missing out on having control of the first impression your business has." - *Online Reviews and Their Impact On the Bottom* Line by Matt Bowman - https://www.forbes.com/sites/forbesagencycouncil/2019/01/15/online-reviews-and-their-impact-on-the-bottom-line/#35d3b4955bde

## NOTABLE QUOTABLE

"Perfectionism is often an excuse for procrastination."

**- PAUL GRAHAM**

(The entrepreneur investor, incubator, and coach behind AirBNB, Dropbox, and Reddit)

_____**Include a compelling 60-second video / commercial (on the top portion above the fold) on your website** to improve your conversion rate. To provide you with an ample example of clients that we have personally worked with who have used a "website header video" in route to dramatically increasing their sales check out:

_____**Create a "top of the website" call to action** that your ideal and likely buyers will relate to and connect with. You want to make it SUPER EASY for your ideal and likely buyers to call you, to schedule an appointment with you, or for them to do business with you in the most convenient way possible. As an AMPLE EXAMPLE check out EITRLounge.com and OXIFresh.com:

144

 **Create a "No-Brainer" sales offer deal** that is so GOOD, so HOT, and so IRRESISTIBLE that your ideal and likely buyers simply cannot resist the urge to at least try out your services and products out. As an example, we would encourage you to check out the following websites.

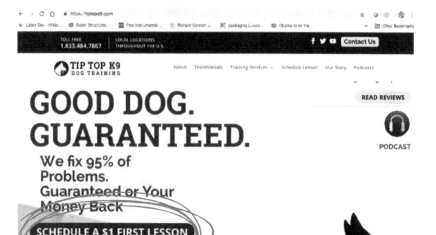

## NOTABLE QUOTABLE

"Genius is 1% inspiration and 99% perspiration."

**- THOMAS EDISON**
(The inventor of the first practical light bulb, recorded audio, recorded video, and the founder of General Electric)

## SUCCESS STORIES 🏆

"Being top in Google has impacted our business tremendously. Knowing that we're top in Google makes it so much easier for our clients to search and if they use certain keywords that pertain to our business, we're the first ones that come up on that page. We get a lot of phone call and website traffic. I would suggest every one takes this program seriously."

**- MYRON KIRKPATRICK**
(Founder of White Glove Auto - WhiteGloveAutoTulsa.com)

# LAWS OF PERSUASION

(How to Apply Pressure to Get Things Done | Do you reject the motive or the method?)

**Definition: Motive**
A reason for doing something, especially one that is hidden or not obvious.

**Definition: Method**
Particular form of procedure for accomplishing or approaching something, especially a systematic or established one.

## WITHOUT THE ABILITY TO PERSUADE PEOPLE YOU CANNOT:

1. Gather reviews
2. Close deals
3. Recruit people
4. Getting a seat at the bar
5. Upselling
6. Deflect the Price Question

## DO YOU REJECT THE MOTIVE OR THE METHOD?

- Guns

- Hiding behind trees

- George Washington was an American politician and soldier who served as the first President of the United States from 1789 to 1797 and was one of the Founding Fathers of the United States. He served as Commander-in-Chief of the Continental Army during the American Revolutionary War,

- Shooting leaders

- Mandatory Inoculation - Smallpox Smallpox was a scourge of the American Colonies, decimating Native American populations and then playing a part in the Revolutionary War. British soldiers had better immunity to the disease than the colonial troops, and may have even used it as a weapon. In 1776, half of the 10,000 Continental Army soldiers around Quebec fell ill with smallpox; of the outbreak, John Adams wrote, "The smallpox is ten times more terrible than the British, Canadians and Indians together. This was the cause of our precipitate retreat from Quebec."

The following year, George Washington, as commander-in-chief of the Continental Army, ordered mandatory inoculation against smallpox for any soldier who had not gained prior immunity against the disease through infection. The procedure in that era was known as variolation, intentionally exposing someone to a mild form of the smallpox virus (Jenner would not develop the smallpox vaccine until 1796). [See related timeline entry.] For the British Army in the North American colonies, inoculation was voluntary.

## BENJAMIN FRANKLIN

Benjamin Franklin was one of the Founding Fathers of the United States. Franklin was a renowned polymath and a leading author, printer, political theorist, politician, freemason, postmaster, scientist, inventor, civic activist, statesman, and diplomat. As a scientist, he was a major figure in the American Enlightenment and the history of physics for his discoveries and theories regarding electricity. As an inventor, he is known for the lightning rod, bifocals, and the Franklin stove, among other inventions.

## ACTION ITEMS:

Motive - It's hard to help a customer you don't have.

- The Law of Communion
- The Law of Effective Rhythm
- The Law of Emotional Transference
- The Laws of Leadership.
- The Law of the Deal Wheel
- The Law of Cheering
- The Law of Success Prioritization
- The Law of Gifting
- The Law of Decision Making
- The Law of Testimonials
- The Law of Self-Fulfilling Prophecies
- The Law of No Drifting
- The Law of Energizing
- The Law of Likability
- Law of Reciprocity
- The Law of Appeal to a Higher Self-Image
- The Law of Contrast
- The Law of the Story Board
- The Law of Commitment and Consistency
- The Law of Scarcity
- The Law of Conflict Avoidance
- The Law of Symbiotic Relationships
- Focus on the Altruistic Goal of Helping Clients Achieve Their Long-term Goal.
- Discover Their Pain and Gain Points
- Master the Art of Timing
- Never Appear too Perfect. Law of Self-Deprecation.
- The Law of Credibility
- The Law of Social Proof
- The Law of Common Union

## HOW TO SET UP GOOGLE MAPS

1. Login to business.google.com

2. Register your address and check the box "service customers at their location" (this hides your physical address)

3. Get the postcard from Google (about 5 days) and enter the code

4. Name your business with business name and keyword you want to rank for. ie. Bob's Gym of Tulsa Gyms

5. Get reviews

6. Get reviews

7. Get some more reviews

8. When you are finished with the last step, get a drink of water and get more reviews

9. Never ever stop getting reviews

## BONUS FUN FACT

According to Forbes, 88% of consumers read reviews before buying.

Behold... the Clark 5 (our kids) pictured above. Success is not about the acquisition of stuff. Success is about being able to have both the time freedom and financial freedom needed to be able to pursue your dreams and visions. Success is about having enough financial resources to be able to spend your time when and where you want to.

RUSH TO REVENUE
Money Cures
All Problems

## $ HOW TO GET CASH FOR YOUR BUSINESS FAST $

1. **Kabbage**

2. **Oklahoma Capital Bank / Regent Bank**

3. **Equity Line**

4. **Walt Disney / Sam Walton Method** (Ask people you know)

5. **Lori Montag (Zany Bands) Method** (Sell your house and put it toward your business)

6. **Nuclear Winter Method** (Fire everyone you do not need)

7. **Clay Clark Method** (Turn your air conditioning and other non-vitals off [cable, dinners out, etc.] to be able to put that money toward the business

## Clay Clark
### THE TENDER YEARS

Look at the size of Clay's 2nd grade melon/dome/cranium/head

Do you see that large human head in the back row? Third from the right? That's me and my huge melon. If I can do it, I know that you can too.

---

## Automate your marketing success!

Create a Marketing Calendar using the STEPPS from Jonah Berger's book *Contagious*

---

Create Approved Social Media Posts for the next year & schedule ALL social media using hootsuite

---

## An SEO Compliant Website Includes:

1. Your website must on an HTML based wordpress website
2. Website must be canonical compliant --> SEMRush.com
3. Every page must have 1,000 words
4. Must create HTML sitemap (what humans see)
5. Must create XML sitemap (what Google sees)
6. Submit website to the Google Search Engine Console
7. Permalinks
8. Meta descriptions
9. Must schedule time to get it done
10. EMBRACE the struggle and schedule the time needed to beat the other guys

\*\*\*
Don't listen to charlatans about SEO who falsely claim to have special secret search engine knowledge that you could not possible understand.
\*\*\*

# The Perfect Converting Landing Pages:

**CHAPTER 9**

# STEP 7

## CREATE A SALES CONVERSION SYSTEM

| Marketing System #1 |

"If you cannot sell, your business will go to hell."

**CLAY CLARK**
*(Father of 5 human kids)*

| Marketing System #2 | Leads | Conversion Call Script / Conversion Text / Conversion Email | Appointment Close |

| Marketing System #3 |

"Call your leads until they cry, die, or buy."

**CLAY CLARK**

Story Time:

Cold Calls, Liquid Courage, The Sports Buzz Radio Show and fighting through anxiety, procrastination, and the fear of failure.

Hear Clay's Story in Person @ the Thrive Conference

RUSH TO REVENUE
Money Cures All Problems

152

"That's been one of my mantras: focus and simplicity. Simple can be harder than complex. You have to work hard to get your thinking clean and make it simple, but it's worth it in the end because once you get there you can move mountains."

**STEVE JOBS**
*Co-founder of Apple and the former CEO of Pixar*

"CREATE A DEFINITE PLAN FOR CARRYING OUT YOUR DESIRE AND BEGIN AT ONCE, WHETHER YOU ARE READY OR NOT, TO PUT THIS PLAN INTO ACTION."
– NAPOLEON HILL
AUTHOR OF "THINK AND GROW RICH"

"When you can't sell your products, services, and goods you'll end up living in the hood."

**CLAY CLARK**
*A man who likes to write rhymes about sales*

##  Story Time: Without Sales You Will Fail

Basically, without sales, all businesses go to hell. In fact, I would guess that approximately 30% of the coaching clients that we have worked with over the years have had an unbelievable product or service or an incredible restaurant, but they just didn't know how to generate sales, how to build sales scripts, how to create a sales funnel, or how to up-sell. You see, the real magic of the Z66 Auto Auction is that every Friday, we are going to sell 1,000 cars and Dr. Zoellner isn't even at the auction half of the time. The real magic with Epic Photography is that each year, thousands of couples book their wedding photos with Epic Photography and I know nothing about photography, but we both know something about selling photography. The real magic with the Doctor Robert Zoellner and Associates Optometry Clinic is that every week, we are going to see hundreds of patients and Dr. Zoellner might not be there. The real magic with the Elephant In The Room Men's Grooming Lounge is that every week, we see hundreds of men and provide them with a haircut and I am not even there.

##  Story Time: The Kanbar Project

Years ago, we were asked to head up the marketing for Kanbar Properties, which you can read about if you do a Google search for Clay Clark and Kanbar, that's K-A-N-B-A-R. The guy who invented Skyy Vodka, Maurice Kanbar, had purchased nearly

29% of downtown Tulsa after selling Skyy Vodka for $600 million and he needed help marketing his properties. Through implementing an intense search engine optimization campaign, a carefully scripted commercial leasing cold call campaign, and a very calculated public relations campaign, Braxton Fears and I were able to lease out nearly one dozen downtown buildings.

RUSH TO REVENUE
Money Cures All Problems

★ ★ ★ ★ ★

# REAL THRIVERS LIKE YOU

"We've gone into overdrive to get Brenda trained. We've had a record month!! We've collected $60,000. We have quite a bit pending insurance as well. Can't wait to finish all the numbers!! That's awesome! Thank you, Clay, for all that you do! We had over 30 leads in March alone!"

*Jennifer Cushman | Office Manager | Face & Body Cosmetic Surgery and Medical Spa*
*www.FaceandBody.net*

"I had the pleasure of working with Mr. Clark in 2010 when I managed over 2.2 million square feet of downtown office and retail space. I can recommend him highly and without reservation. I had hired Mr. Clark to re-brand the portfolio, and to reach out to prospective tenants. Throughout the course of the campaign, Mr. Clark was a consummate professional. He conducted market research, built a web-site, and coordinated obtaining pictures, print materials, and gaining media attention with-in what I would deem record time. Within the first week of Mr. Clark going public with the campaign, he generated hundreds of prospective tenants. Mr. Clark's positive attitude is contagious, he is hard worker, and he is genuinely a great guy to work with. I hope that in the near future I will have the opportunity to work with Mr. Clark again."

**DAVID ATKINSON**
*Former Vice President of Kanbar Properties*

---

### Deep Thoughts

**"My product is so good it will sell itself."**

**SOMEONE WHO IS POOR**
*(Or who is about to become poor)*

---

RUSH TO REVENUE
Money Cures All Problems

# SYSTEMATIC SALES CHECKLIST

1. Create an inbound sales script.

2. Create an outbound sales script.

3. Create pre-written sales emails.

4. Create pre-written sales texts.

5. Create sales one sheet.

6. Create pre-written sales / presentation book.

7. Create pre-written presentation script.

8. Create sales FAQ sheet related to the questions asked by your ideal and likely buyers.

9. Create sales manual.

10. Print, review, and post deal wheel method at every sales station.

11. Create a documented sales workflow using a white-board.

12. Create a lead tracker spreadsheet.

**Find Script templates at** ThriveTimeShow.com/resources

# SALES SYSTEM CREATION SUPER MOVES

1.  **Download the Legendary Deal Wheel and a sample Sales Script Template at ThriveTimeShow.com today.**

2.  **Create sales training videos documenting the proven system.**

3.  **Create a lead organization system:**

- Bin for hot leads (leads that have reached out to your business requesting additional information about the products and services that your company provides)

- Bin for appointments

- Bin for missed appointments

- Bin for cold leads (leads secured from lists, trade shows, etc.)

4.  **Record all calls using ClarityVoice.com or 8x8 - http://www.ClarityVoice.com/ 8x8 - https://www.8x8.com/**

5.  **Tape-a-Call for Mobile**

6.  **Similar to watching game film, taste testing, or calibrating equipment!**

Sales Scripting 101

- **Rapport** – Script 5 Questions
- **Needs** – Script 5 Questions
- **Benefits** – Script 5 benefits supported by facts
- **Close** – Script 5 Closing Questions
- **Isolate Objections**

RUSH TO REVENUE
Money Cures All Problems

## DAILY SALES KEY PERFORMANCE INDICATORS

1. How many outbound calls were made?

2. How many appointments were made?

3. How many deals were closed?

4. Why did people say no?

---

Base Sales KPI's on the super Star Sales person, not the average in the group.

---

Keep team accountable to KPI's with short, daily standing meetings.

"You don't have to be a doctor to build a sales focused culture. However, you do need a PHD: Pig-Headed Discipline."

**CLAY CLARK**
*Co-Host of the ThriveTime Business Coach Radio Show and member of the Forbes Coaches Council*

158

Invest the time needed to build repeatable sales systems today so that you can focus on what really matters. You can do this.

"People who are unable to motivate themselves must be content with mediocrity, no matter how impressive their other talents."

**ANDREW CARNEGIE**
*The man who built the Carnegie Steel Company, sold it to J.P. Morgan for $480 million, and spent the later part of his life dedicated to philanthropy*

"When you created a bunch of products and you can't sell any you'll soon find yourself eating dog food and being surrounded by kids who are skinny."

**CLAY TIBERIUS CLARK**
*Self-proclaimed winner of the most humble man in the world award*

**CHAPTER 10**

# STEP 8

## DETERMINE SUSTAINABLE CUSTOMER ACQUISITION COSTS

$127          $37          $52          ???

Meet the Customer Types:

- Apostle
- Loyalist
- Mercenary

- Hostage
- Terrorist

"There is a strong chance that no one will wake up with a burning desire to pay you. If you can't sell, you can't generate word of mouth and your business will go to hell."

**CLAY CLARK**
*Me, the father of 5 human kids, and the former U.S. Small Business Administration Entrepreneur of the Year*

##  Story Time: Growing America's Largest Wedding Entertainment Business

This is the part of business that both Dr. Zoellner and I are obsessed with. For my first business, DJConnection.com, once I was able to create a turn-key system to market to brides and to book their weddings for $57 per confirmed customer, it was off to the races and scaling the business. We just have to help you figure out which marketing is going to produce the best results for you and how much it is going to cost you to acquire each new customer. After that, the word-of-mouth marketing will begin to take over as long as you have a good product and provide a great customer service experience.

##  Story Time: Growing A Dental Practice

Recently I worked with a dentist and we got his cost per confirmed booking down to just under $100 per confirmed paying customer. For this business, this is great because an orthodontist will typically profit over $2,000 per patient after expenses.

 Braxton Fears and I actually started a commercial real estate business to fund the achievement of our life goals. With no previous experience in the industry, we got our cost per confirmed commercial real estate listing to under $150 per listing. Before we dropped the mic and Braxton went back into ministry full-time, we were able to scale up the business in just under three years.

# REAL THRIVERS LIKE YOU

"Clay Clark has been instrumental in providing me with business guidance at the right times! He has moved both of my companies to the top of Google searches and helped me to be featured in countless media outlets and publications. I have a big vision in what God has called me to do and sometimes as an entrepreneur you can dream so big that you can lose focus. With three successful companies, I knew that it was time for growth and sustainability so that we could reach the people that we needed to reach. I truly believe that God brings certain people into your life at certain times and I thank God for bringing Clay at a time of need. Clay has been instrumental in combining his business savvy with my big vision. The bottom line is that I am in business to help people...but I am also in business to make money, and that is what Clay has helped me do! If you are considering bringing Clay on for anything business related, it will be the best investment you ever make."

*Jonathan Conneely | "Coach JC" | Founder / President | JJC Enterprises*

## Story Time: $23 Million of Sales in One Year

"It's wife bragging time. (Because I know she won't do it herself...) We started Sprik Realty just over a year ago. Which means 2016 is our first full calendar year. Numbers are in for the year and I couldn't be more proud. Over $23 million in sales for the year!! Awesome job all of the agents have done. Many were new in 2016 and are just beginning to hit their stride. 2017 is going to be AWESOME!! Congrats Danielle Sitcler Sprik and all the Sprik Agents. Keep doing what you do."

**TIM SPRIK**
*Co-founder of Sprik Realty*

# MARKETING & ADVERTISING SUPER PLAYS

Write down each type of marketing / advertising you are currently doing and the amount of sales generated as a result of this marketing / advertising effort:

Divide the amount spent weekly on advertising by the number of closed deals.

| Current Marketing: | Amount Spent: | Total Revenue Generated: |
|---|---|---|
| _____ | _____ | _____ |
| _____ | _____ | _____ |
| _____ | _____ | _____ |
| _____ | _____ | _____ |
| _____ | _____ | _____ |
| _____ | _____ | _____ |
| _____ | _____ | _____ |
| _____ | _____ | _____ |
| _____ | _____ | _____ |
| _____ | _____ | _____ |
| _____ | _____ | _____ |
| _____ | _____ | _____ |
| _____ | _____ | _____ |

"He who cannot sell must work for someone who can."

**CLAY CLARK**
*The founder of DJ Connection, Epic Photos, ThriveTimeShow.com, The Make Your Life Epic Agency, etc.*

"MOST ENTREPRENEURS ARE MERELY TECHNICIANS WITH AN ENTREPRENEURIAL SEIZURE. MOST ENTREPRENEURS FAIL BECAUSE THEY ARE WORKING IN THEIR BUSINESS RATHER THAN ON THEIR BUSINESS."
- MICHAEL GERBER
AUTHOR OF "THE E-MYTH REVISITED"

# EMOTIONAL ROLLER COASTER CHECK

Don't freak out if your initial marketing attempts are not producing immediate fruit. As an entrepreneur, you must absolutely be sold out to the rhythm of: DEFINE, ACT, MEASURE, REFINE. Don't remain loyal to a type of advertising because your wife's boss sold it to you or because just have a deep seated and insatiable love for the Yellow Pages.

- Define what you think is going to work with your coach.

- Act after you have gathered all of the facts.

- Measure the results of the action steps that you have taken without bias.

- Refine the actions you are taking until you begin to produce the results you are looking for.

*"TEMPORARY FAILURES ARE A PREREQUISITE TO SUCCESS."*
*—NAPOLEON HILL*
*BEST-SELLING SUCCESS AUTHOR OF "THINK AND GROW RICH"*

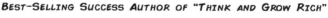

★ ★ ★ ★ ★

# REAL THRIVERS LIKE YOU

"I have come to realize that foundational sales principles work, regardless of what you're selling. I work at a coffee shop and my boss told me 'Hey, we really need to sell more coffee beans.' So I started employing the creative use of imagery, humor, phrasing and tried and true sales methods taught to me by Clay Clark and the book he recommended I read, Soft Selling in a Hard World. I made posters describing the different coffees with funny pop culture references along with legitimate consumer reviews of each coffee. I also began using 'the 90-second close.' Our store shot up to the spot of #1 in whole bean sales out of 613 stores in our entire region. Not only that, but we are averaging 5 pounds sold out of every 100 customers that come into the store, whereas the average store in the US sees 1 to 1.5 pounds sold per every 100 customers that come in. These numbers don't lie and they just point to the fact that a proper training in sales by someone who knows what they are doing and who has a track record to prove it can make you succeed in sales in whatever business realm you find yourself in, even the coffee shop business."

*Scott T. | Store Manager & Barista | Starbucks Coffee*

"Ninety-nine percent of all failures come from people who have a habit of making excuses."

**GEORGE WASHINGTON CARVER**
*The man who was born a slave who went onto become a world-class inventor, botanist and entrepreneur*

RUSH TO REVENUE
Money Cures All Problems

## Subscribe to the ThriveTimeShow.com Podcast Today
### And Receive a FREE Fist Bump from Clay Clark!*

*This will be a virtual fist bump. For a real fist bump, attend our Business Workshop at the ThriveTime Show Headquarters in beautiful Jenks, Oklahoma!*

# CHAPTER 11

# STEP 9

## CREATE REPEATABLE SYSTEMS, PROCESSES, AND FILE ORGANIZATION

"Once you have built repeatable and profitable systems, you will discover that you have built a time freedom and financial freedom creating business that serves you and not an overwhelming job."

**CLAY CLARK**
*Former U.S. SBA Entrepreneur of the Year*

"Systems permit ordinary people to achieve extraordinary results."

**MICHAEL GERBER**
*The best-selling author of the E-Myth book series*

**ABBREVIATIONS ELONGATE EVERYTHING**

RUSH TO REVENUE
Money Cures All Problems

## TRAINING CHECKLIST / PROCESS CREATION

1. You Tell them
2. You Show Them

3. They Show You
4. They Demonstrate Mastery

"Simplicity is the ultimate sophistication."

**STEVE JOBS**
*Co-Founder of Apple*

Most coaching clients that we work with have told us that they used to struggle in this area because they believe that their industry is so different and that you can't possibly turn their service or product into a repeatable system. However, through obsessing about their workflows, checklists, and systems, Dr. Zoellner and I have been able to build scalable optometry clinics, diagnostic sleep centers, wedding photography businesses, marketing firms, auto auctions, fitness companies, and a successful business in a ridiculous amount of industries. We are always preaching that repeatable systems are the tools of the titans. People who can't wrap their minds around this concept are really just technicians who are skilled in one area but are pretending to be entrepreneurs. You want to build a business, not a job.

"Most entrepreneurs are merely technicians with an entrepreneurial seizure. Most entrepreneurs fail because you are working IN your business rather than ON your business."

**MICHAEL GERBER**
*Best-selling author of the E-Myth revisited book series*

RUSH TO REVENUE
Money Cures All Problems

Once you have invested the time and money into building world-class business systems they will not work unless you take the 5 following action steps:

1. Trust but verify everything and everybody
2. Always create a followup loop
3. Hire consistant Mystery Shoppers
4. Create a pipeline of inbound new people
5. Fire when ready

## MAKE IT REPEATABLE

## 7 SUPER PLAYS FOR SYSTEMIZING YOUR SUCCESS

1. Write out all repetitive tasks that you and your team have to do over and over to deliver what your customers have paid you for.

_____

_____

_____

_____

2. Write out all of the repetitive marketing tasks that you and your team have to do to generate sales.

_____

_____

_____

_____

3. Write out all of the repetitive customer service related tasks that you and your team have to respond to on a daily basis.

_____

_____

_____

_____

"If you want to end up with a career as a hobo, have a bunch of meetings to talk about your feelings and make sure that your sales totals are low."

**CLAY CLARK**
_A man obsessed with the New England Patriots_

4. Write out all of the repetitive accounting related tasks that you and your team have to do on a daily basis to keep up with your numbers.

_____

_____

_____

_____

5. Write out all of the repetitive human resources tasks that you and your team have to do on a daily basis to bring in the talent you rely on to operate your business.

_____

_____

_____

_____

6. Write out all of your biggest limiting factors.

_____

_____

_____

_____

7. Write out all of your smallest limiting factors.

_____

_____

_____

_____

RUSH TO REVENUE
Money Cures All Problems

Journal out your next week of work and where you are currently investing your time on a daily basis.

_____

_____

_____

_____

_____

_____

_____

_____

_____

_____

_____

_____

_____

_____

_____

_____

_____

_____

_____

_____

_____

_____

_____

**Create a Standardized Naming Scheme for All Documents and Files**

**Keep all files stores on Dropbox**

# Create a Checklist & Process for Every Step of Workflow Mapping

THIS
IS WHY
WE DO IT

PRESENTATION LAYER
HOW IT'S COMMUNICATED

PROCESS LAYER
THE WHAT

You can create profits that wow when you invest the time to build repeatable business systems. Remember...the end goal of starting a business is to create both time and financial freedom.

# The Perfect Meeting Agenda

**Transition into "Reporting Mode"**
15:min

1. Review Scorecard - Make sure scorecard numbers are on track. *(5 minutes)*
2. Rock Review - Make sure priorities are on track. *(5 minutes)*
3. Customer or Employee Headlines - Share good and bad news in one sentence headlines to keep everyone informed about what is going on with all of your people.

If there are any scoreboard discrepancies, priority issues or headlines that need to be addressed, those items should be added to the "Issues List."

**Review To-Do List**

These are 7-day action items. Review last week's list to ensure that they are complete.
**RULE OF THUMB:** 90% of the to-do list should be getting done each week.

 **IDS (Identify, Discuss, Solve). Issue-Solving Track**
60:min

Some weeks you may only get through one issue, other weeks you may get through ten, but as long as you are taking them in order of priority you are doing the right thing.

Load up your issues list and then prioritize those items based on what is the 1st, 2nd and 3rd most urgent isssue. If everything is of the importance, nothing gets done. Tackle each item on the list using Gino Wickman's system of indentifying, discussing and solving the issue.

1. Identify the real issue. Dive in and really find the true problem before the problem solving begins.
2. Begin discussing the issue with a spirit of candor. Attack the problem, not the people.
3. The entire focus must be on problem solving. Once you solve the problem, schedule the action steps on the "to-do list"

**Meeting Conclusion**

1. Recap the to-do list.
2. Discuss any messages that need to be shared out to the rest of the company.
3. Quickly rate your meeting on how you did today from 1-10 (10 being best.) 8 is the minimum standard. If you are not reaching an 8, discuss why and begin to self correct.

*Note: To learn more about how to construct the agenda and outline for a perfect meeting read "Traction" by Gino Wickman.*

> "I would prefer not to focus on sales, I'd rather put my focus on developing a great product."

**A STARVING WANTREPRENEUR**
*Someone who is definitely not you and who you definitely don't want to be*

**CHAPTER 12**

# STEP 10

## MANAGEMENT
## EXECUTION

"If you pick the right people and give them the opportunity to spread their wings and put compensation as a carrier behind it you almost don't have to manage them."

**JACK WELCH**
*The former CEO of GE who grew the company by 4,000% during his tenure*

"Management consists of your ability to get the members of your team to execute your business plans, systems and processes with excellence."

**CLAY CLARK**
*The Father of 5 Kids and Man-bear-pig*

## Action Items:

1. What is your process for hiring people?

2. What is your process for inspiring people?

3. What is your process for firing people?

Having coached businesses all over the world, we often see two very predictable forms of dysfunction arise once the systems have been built and it comes from the daily management and execution of the business systems. The first problem we consistently see is the owner of the business failing to get their work done and the second problem we see is the team failing to get their work done. Typically, the justification for not getting work done involves somebody saying, "I ran out of time." This on the surface may sound like a valid excuse, but your business and your success matters too much for us to just accept this excuse as being valid. My friend, we are going to dramatically grow your time and financial freedom and in order to do that, you must learn how to create the time in your schedule needed to get things done and create a culture of accountability.

"One of the first and maybe most important parts of a good time-management system is to take the time every single day to do Planning Time. You must plan your day just like you plan your vacation. You would not wake up in the morning and go on vacation without a plan and driving without a map. Don't head off every morning with no plan. With no map you will not get where you want to go, and with no plan you may not even know where you want to go. This simply means that you need to take anywhere from 30 minutes to a few minutes every day to think about what you need to get done today, this week, this month-and if you are really great at planning—this year and the years to follow."

**LEE COCKERELL**
*Thrive15.com partner and mentor and the former Executive Vice President of Walt Disney World Resorts who used to manage 40,000 employees*

Hear Clay's Story in Person @ the Thrive Conference

Story Time:

Delegate everything that is not your highest and best use if possible. The dangers of making your own bio-diesel.

RUSH TO REVENUE
Money Cures All Problems

Henceforth, you, my friend, are going to need to schedule "META-TIME," "Quiet Time", or "Planning Time" into your daily schedule. What does "META-TIME" mean? Meta is a Greek word that means "above or beyond." Essentially, you must schedule time to work "above" your business, "beyond" your daily reactive problems, and "on" your business, not just in it. You must find both a consistent time and place to think about your business and your life and where you are versus where you want to be. You want to have an hour blocked out in your schedule where you phone is off, your email is off, your social media is off, your text messages are off, all notifications are off, and nobody can reach you because soon, this will be the SINGLE MOST VALUABLE AND IMPORTANT PART OF YOUR DAY.

Some entrepreneurs prefer getting up early to find their "Meta Time" and some entrepreneurs find that staying up late is what works best for them. Because I have 5 kids, 40 chickens, 4 cats, 9 businesses, 1 radio show and a lot going on... I find that the morning time in my "Man Cave" is the only time that works for me for my consistent "Meta Time." In fact, I'm writing this book right now, at 3:40 AM during my personal "Meta Time." Because this book is all about you, the big questions that now remain are:

**1.** When will your daily meta-time be?

_____

**2.** Where will your daily meta-time take place?

_____

**3.** What do you need to have with you to make this time the most productive it can be? (computer, pen, pad of paper, stapler, 3 monitors and a computer, etc.)

_____

Holding your organization accountable starts with you holding yourself accountable, but then once you've mastered that, you are going to have to become very comfortable with holding your team accountable. And your team, like all teams, will naturally drift by default and it's your job to hold your team accountable to execute these business systems that you have built. And holding people accountable always requires uncomfortable conversations.

"EXPECT MORE THAN OTHERS THINK POSSIBLE."
— HOWARD SCHULTZ
FOUNDER OF STARBUCKS

"A person's success in life can usually be measured by the number of uncomfortable conversations he or she is willing to have."

**TIM FERRISS**
*Best-selling author of the Four Hour Work Week, former startup venture capitalist, and award-winning podcaster*

"Some people aren't used to an environment where excellence is expected."

**STEVE JOBS**
*The co-founder of Apple and the former CEO of PIXAR*

## SUPER PLAYS

1. Never assign action items or hold people accountable over e-mail.

2. Never assign action items or hold people accountable over text.

RUSH TO REVENUE
Money Cures All Problems

★ ★ ★ ★ ★

# REAL THRIVERS LIKE YOU

"Clay, I just want you to know that this last year has been unbelievable. I've gone from poverty thinking to just a small measure of wealth thinking and, as the book said, the universe has discovered me!!! I've never felt so free! I truly have become what T. Harv Eker calls, 'a money magnet'! And it's only the beginning. We have seven revenue streams now and each of them are growing and contributing daily. Thank you Clay Clark! My life is expanding and you have been a major influence on me! Have a great day, my friend!"

*Clay Staires | Professional Speaker/Trainer and Growth Expert | The Leadership Initiative*
*www.claystaires.com*

"Steve Jobs has a saying that A players hire A players; B players hire C players; and C players hire D players. It doesn't take long to get to Z players. This trickle-down effect causes bozo explosions in companies."

**GUY KAWASAKI**
*An American marketing specialist, author, and Silicon Valley venture capitalist. He was one of the Apple employees originally responsible for marketing their Macintosh computer line in 1984*

"We believe that it's really important to come up with core values that you can commit to. And by commit, we mean that you're willing to hire and fire based on them. If you're willing to do that, then you're well on your way to building a company culture that is in line with the brand you want to build."

**TONY HSIEH**
*CEO of Zappos*

RUSH TO REVENUE
Money Cures All Problems

> "One lesson I learned [at PayPal] is to fire people faster. That sounds awful, but I think if somebody is not working out, it's best to part ways sooner rather than later. It's a mistake to try too hard to make something work that really couldn't work."

**ELON MUSK**

*The founder, CEO, and CTO of SpaceX; co-founder, CEO, and product architect of Tesla Motors; co-founder and chairman of SolarCity; co-chairman of OpenAI; co-founder of Zip2; and founder of X.com which merged with PayPal of Confinity*

"CONTROL YOUR OWN DESTINY OR
SOMEONE ELSE WILL."
- JACK WELCH
FORMER CEO OF GENERAL ELECTRIC

The former marketing guru for Apple, Guy Kawasaki, said it best when he said, "Ideas are easy. Execution is difficult." Thomas Edison piled on when he said, "Vision without execution is hallucination." Back in the day, the Titan himself, John D. Rockefeller, once said, "The ability to deal with people is as purchasable a commodity as sugar or coffee and I will pay more for that ability than for any other under the sun."

## 📖 Story Time: How to Become a Master of Management

Doctor Zoellner and I have learned to become masters of management because we know the performance and the key performance indicators that we need out of each position on the team and we hold our teams accountable for it on a daily basis. We don't feel bad when an employee fails to meet the expectations that we have clearly laid out for them. Now, because we have hundreds of employees between the two of us, we have hired a great team of results focused managers who hold people accountable for getting stuff done even when team members don't feel like it. Because we never stop doing the group interview every week for every position, we have a steady stream of new recruits coming in to replace those that don't make the cut and get fired.

"There is only one boss. The customer. And he can fire everybody in the company from the chairman on down, simply by spending his money somewhere else."

**SAM WALTON**
*An American businessman and entrepreneur best known for founding the retailers Walmart and Sam's Club*

"Say no to poverty. Say yes to sales."

**CLAY CLARK**
*A man with an obsession for burning pinion wood.*

★ ★ ★ ★ ★

# REAL THRIVERS LIKE YOU

"Clay is the best emcee and entertainer we have ever used. From the time the first guest walked into the room until the last guest left, you electrified the room with your energy! Thank you for taking our event to the NEXT LEVEL (as you like to say)!"

*Angie W. | Event Planning Team | 11th Annual Zenith Awards | Apartment Association*

"FACE REALITY AS IT IS, NOT AS IT WAS
OR AS YOU WISH IT TO BE."
- JACK WELCH
FORMER CEO OF GENERAL ELECTRIC

"Without candor, everyone saved face, and business lumbered along. The status quo was accepted. Fake behavior was just a day at the office. And people with initiative, gumption, and guts were labeled troublesome—or worse...Now for the really bad news. Even though candor is vital to winning, it is hard and time-consuming to instill in any group, no matter what size...To get candor, you reward it, praise it, and talk about it. You make public heroes out of people who demonstrate it. Most of all, you yourself demonstrate it in an exuberant and even exaggerated way—even when you're not the boss."

**JACK WELCH**
*Arguably the most successful CEO in the history of American business. The former CEO of GE.*

Story Time:

The permanent substitute teacher Mr. Anderson. The Boys choir. Rotten fish and Lyrical Miracles.

Hear Clay's Story in Person @ the Thrive Conference

RUSH TO REVENUE
Money Cures All Problems

# THE "KEEPING YOUR TEAM ON TRACK" CHECKLIST

Write out when you will do the daily huddles with your team to keep them on track.

Write out the key performance indicators that you will hold each member accountable for.

Write out a list of the daily action items that are not getting done at your business but should be. Create daily checklists for each of the jobs within your business.

Work with your coach to develop a merit-based pay system for your team based upon paying people for what they do vs. what they say they are going to do.

**Position:**

_____

**Pay:**

_____

**Metric / Key Performance Indicators:**

_____

**Carrot:**

_____

**Stick:**

_____

Create a list of all of your employees.

Label all employees as either A, B or C players (talk to your coach if you get stuck).

Block out time to train up your team members on a weekly basis.

Work with your coach to develop job descriptions for all of the positions within your business.

Schedule time into your schedule for your weekly group interviews (go over this concept with your coach).

Every week: Launch hiring advertisements (On Craigslist, Monster.com and Indeed.com) to promote job openings before they are open. This way you are not stuck dealing with dysfunctional employees.

Commit to firing / replacing the bottom 10% of your employee roster if they show themselves to be unwilling to improve.

Let team members know that you are focused on the growth of the company and their personal growth. Then begin kicking, hugging, documenting and pruning as needed.

"When you don't focus on making products and services that will sell the rest of your entrepreneurial experience won't go well."

**CLAY CLARK**
*A man who has been self employed since age 16*

# RANK YOUR TEAM

A Players:

_____

_____

_____

B Players:

_____

_____

_____

C Players:

_____

_____

_____

"You can't manage like a socialist in a Capitalist Economy. Protecting under performers always backfires. The worst thing though, is how protecting people who don't perform hurts the people themselves."

**JACK WELCH**
*Legendary CEO of GE who grew the company 4,000%*

RUSH TO
REVENUE
Money Cures
All Problems

**CHAPTER 13**

# STEP 11

## CREATE A SUSTAINABLE AND
## REPETITIVE WEEKLY SCHEDULE

"The secret to success is determined by your daily agenda."

**JOHN MAXWELL**
*Former pastor and best selling author of The 21 Irrefutable Laws of Leadership.*

Sample of the F6 Journal designed by Clay Clark for Entrepreneurs like you.

"The goal is to be able to live your life the way Michael Jordan played basketball or Marvin Gaye sang a song. To be able to feel the way you feel when you laugh at a joke but to feel that way all the time."

**RUSSELL SIMMONS**
*An American entrepreneur, producer, and author. The Chairman and CEO of Rush Communications, he co-founded the hip-hop music label Def Jam Recordings and created the clothing fashion line, Phat Farm*

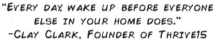

"EVERY DAY, WAKE UP BEFORE EVERYONE ELSE IN YOUR HOME DOES."
-CLAY CLARK, FOUNDER OF THRIVE15

This part is really hard for most entrepreneurs because they really enjoy their jobs. However, there is more to life than just working. In fact, the F6 philosophy is at the center of our entire mission to mentor millions and help you build repeatable business systems that are capable of helping you to produce both the time and financial freedom that you want.

"Remembering that I'll be dead soon is the most important tool I've ever encountered to help me make the big choices in life. Almost everything--all external expectations, all pride, all fear of embarrassment or failure--these things just fall away in the face of death, leaving only what is truly important. Remembering that you are going to die is the best way I know to avoid the trap of thinking you have something to lose. You are already naked. There is no reason not to follow your heart. No one wants to die. Even people who want to go to heaven don't want to die to get there. And yet, death is the destination we all share. No one has ever escaped it, and that is how it should be, because death is very likely the single best invention of life. It's life's change agent. It clears out the old to make way for the new."

**STEVE JOBS**
*Co-founder of Apple and former CEO of PIXAR*

### If You Had One Year Left To Live, What Would You Spend Your Time Doing?

_____

_____

_____

_____

_____

_____

RUSH TO REVENUE
*Money Cures All Problems*

*MORE PEOPLE WILL YELL AND WAVE AT YOU TO TELL YOU THAT YOU FORGOT TO CLOSE YOUR GAS CAP THAN THE AMOUNT OF PEOPLE WHO WILL STOP TO TELL YOU THAT YOU ARE GOING THE WRONG DIRECTION WITH YOUR LIFE.*

## Schedule Time to Live the Life You Want!.

Our business partner and the man who used to manage Walt Disney World Resorts and the 40,000 employees who worked there once said, "Only what is scheduled gets done." Basically, you have to schedule time into your calendar for your faith, your family, your friendships, your fitness, and your finances or you will naturally drift.

Napoleon Hill, the best-selling self-help author of all-time and the former apprentice of Andrew Carnegie once said, if you don't have specific goals and "If you have no major purpose, you are drifting toward certain failure." You have to be very intentional about designing a schedule that works for both you and your family. Be specific. Keep it up to date and if something isn't working in it, be sure to make adjustments.

## Story Time: Golfing Enthusiasts Who Schedule Time to Golf are Happier

Years ago, we worked with a client who loved golfing with a passion. This guy was obsessed with golf. However, as his business grew he began missing his weekly golfing tee times. Then because he felt bad about cancelling his tee times, he quit golfing all together. When we sat down with him and really analyzed what made him happy, it was clear that he needed to schedule time to go golfing every week in order for him to truly love his time spent on this planet. Once he scheduled golf back into his weekly schedule, his work performance improved, he got in better physical shape, and his energy level was higher. This small change made a big impact on his overall level of happiness.

RUSH TO REVENUE
Money Cures All Problems

# BLOCK OUT TIME FOR ACTIVITIES YOU WANT TO DO

1. Write out the activities that you love doing and that you would love doing more often if you "just had the time."

2. Schedule and block out times for the pursuit and development of your faith, family, friendships, fitness, finances, and fun into your weekly schedule.

3. Work with your coach to find the time to do what you love if you truly can't seem to find the time for yourself.

4. Setup an email optimization system (one inbox).

5. Setup a calendar optimization system (one master calendar).

6. Setup an action item to-do list system.

7. Schedule daily follow up times with direct reports.

It's not about where you came from or what kind of car you are driving today. It's about where you are going. I started my entrepreneurial journey inside a 1989 Ford Escort.

# What do you enjoy doing?

Faith related activities: _____

Family related activities: _____

Friendship related activites: _____

Fitness related activities:_____

Finance related activites:_____

# Stumped?
# Tips on having fun

1. Watch every New England Patriots game

2. Draw a picture of Tom Brady

3. Attend a Patriots game

4. Buy "Do Your Job: A Look Under the Hoodie of Belichick"

CHAPTER 14

# STEP 12

## HUMAN RESOURCES AND RECRUITMENT

"A small team of A+ players can run circles around a giant team of B and C players."

**STEVE JOBS**
*Co-founder of Apple and former CEO of PIXAR*

"If you pick the right people and give them the opportunity to spread their wings and put compensation as a carrier behind it you almost don't have to manage them."

**JACK WELCH**
*Former CEO of GE, who many argue is the most successful CEO in the history of American business*

## 75% OF EMPLOYEES STEAL

Unfortunately, according to the study the U.S. Chamber did in conjunction with CBS News, they found that over 75% of employees steal from the workplace and most do so repeatedly. In fact, Gallup showed 70% of U.S. workers not engaged at work. Forbes has reported that the number of people who admit to wasting time at work every day has now reached a whopping 89%.

*http://www.cbsnews.com/news/employee-theft-are-you-blind-to-it/*

If you can't find, hire, inspire, and train good people, nothing will work. The good news is that Doctor Zoellner now employs 8 optometrists and EpicPhotos.com is now able to find and train over 40 photographers per week who can go out there and deliver award-winning photography.

Story Time:

Stanford and the coder of who couldn't code.

Hear Clay's Story in Person @ the Thrive Conference

RUSH TO REVENUE
Money Cures All Problems

# REAL THRIVERS LIKE YOU

"Wow. Wow. Wow. Thank you for your input and for working so hard for me behind the scenes while we were back and forth for this (for the TV show, "The Voice"). I'm humbled and overwhelmed with gratitude. So glad to know you and your sweet family. Thanks for believing in me!"

*Amanda Preslar | Founder of PreslarMusic.com*

 ## Story Time: Fire Those Who Cannot Inspire

At the Make Your Life Epic Advertising and Marketing Agency (www. MakeYourLifeEpic.com), we realistically fire one person every other week for failing to show up to work on time consistently, for not doing their job, or for something dumb that they are doing. However, we are not stuck with these people because we have systems in place that bring in a steady pipeline of good people. Once we learned how to systematically find good people, we could start pulling the weeds, firing the horrible employees, and executing on all of the business systems that we are going to help you build too.

 ## Story Time: The Quest for Quality Carpet Cleaners

One of the biggest carpet cleaning franchises on the planet is called Oxi Fresh. The founder of the company, Jonathan Barnett, is one of my business partners at Elephant In The Room. He, just like every business owner, eventually found that their biggest limiting factor was their ability to help their franchisees to find diligent technicians who were willing to clean carpets on-time and professionally all the while demonstrating respect for the homes of the clients they were working with. Through the implementation of consistent weekly job posts, weekly interviews, and a compelling website, they were able to build systems that now sustainably allows them to hire and train enough technicians to keep up with the demand for their services.

RUSH TO REVENUE
Money Cures All Problems

# YOU WILL NOT LET THE FOLLOWING EXCUSES LIMIT YOUR GROWTH

At the Z66 Auto Auction, Epic Photography, The Make Your Life Epic Marketing Agency, the Elephant In The Room Men's Grooming Lounge, and Doctor Robert Zoellner and Associates, we could have the following super-weak alibis that most unsuccessful business owners would pile on to and say "YOU ARE RIGHT." Take a moment and circle the following excuses that you are committing to not make for yourself and your company as you go out there and attempt to find good team members to find, hire, inspire, and hold accountable.

## Excuses

1. It's just hard to find good people who have experience working with _____ (auto title work, photography, men's grooming).

2. It's too hard to find bilingual people who have experience working with _____ (auto title processing, photography, men's grooming).

3. It's too hard to find emotionally stable _____ (hair stylists, photographers, doctors, etc.).

4. It's too hard to find good millennial employees who are willing to do _____ (photography, men's grooming, auto sales, etc.).

5. It's very hard to find skilled _____ (doctors, nurses, technicians, mechanics, photographers, etc.) who are willing to work on the weekends.

6. It's impossible to find good _____ (doctors, nurses, technicians, hair stylists) who are not on drugs.

RUSH TO REVENUE
Money Cures All Problems

7. It's not even possible to find _____ (mechanics, doctors, photographers, hair stylists, etc.) who understand the concept of time management.

8. It's too hard to find good people these days, so we just can't grow.

9. There is a huge shortage of tradesmen in America today.

10. You can't find good _____ (mechanics, photographers, doctors, nurses, salespeople, optometrists) who are humble and trainable.

11. You can't find people who are willing to work on weekends.

12. It's very hard and nearly impossible to find people who are willing to manage a store that is open 7 days per week.

13. Most candidates are not a good fit, so we stopped looking.

## The 11 Step People Finding Process

1. Create a "Now Hiring" Graphic based on the ThriveTime Show Best Practice Using Your Company Branding

2. Schedule Weekly Time to Post on Job Boards

3. Create Group Interview Email Response

4. Respond to All Candidate Applications Via Email

5. Hold Group Interviews Using Group Interview Outline

6. Invite Qualified Candidates to Shadow

7. Create an Employee Handbook

8. Create an On-boarding Checklist

9. Design an Organizational Chart Using Company Branding

10. Create an Employee Skills Mastery Checklist

11. Create an Employee Write-Up System

## The 2 Step People Firing Process

1. Write people up immediately when issues occur

2. Do not engage with criers, liars, excuse makers, or thieves. Just say "It is not working out."

Are you forgetting something?
If you don't schedule and block
out time to get something done
it won't get done. What gets
scheduled gets done.

Find Proven
Templates at
ThriveTimeShow.com/resources

## Subscribe to the ThriveTime Show Podcast today to experience Business School WITHOUT the B.S.!

**CHAPTER 15**

# STEP 13

## DO YOUR ACCOUNTING

"A budget is telling your money where to go instead of wondering where it went."

**DAVE RAMSEY**
*Best selling author and radio talk show host*

## 2 STEPS

to becoming a millionaire in the next 20 years without ever acheiving a big win, winning the jackpot, befriending a leprechaun, riding a unicorn, joining a pyramid scheme, joining a ponzi scheme, going viral or building a hugely succesful business.

1.  Meet with a financial advisor and automate your pre-tax investing in an individual retirement account (IRA), or a Roth Individual Retirement Account.

2.  Avoid Death for the next 20 years. (Stop, drop and roll. Look both ways before crossing traffic, Don't text and drive. Wear a helmet at all times. Eat organic. Don't smoke. Say no to drugs.

RUSH TO REVENUE
Money Cures All Problems

# REAL THRIVERS LIKE YOU

"So far we've generated $63,600 of additional annual gross revenue as a result of the ACCESS plan you helped us create. We are closing in on $10K in monthly revenue. I just signed up an additional ACCESS client and it's the 2nd one that I've landed in the last 30 days from LinkedIn. And the only thing I'm doing on LinkedIn is the Myth versus Law and the Legal Mumbo Jumbo. I'm not doing any other activity. So that appears to really be working in that medium. So I'm making $850 a month off of my free LinkedIn subscription. So I'm kind of excited. So I just wanted to let you know that some of what we are doing is working."

*Scott Reib | Attorney at Law*
*ReibLaw.com*

"What gets measured gets done."

**GINO WICKMAN**
*Best-selling author of Traction*

## DON'T BE AVERAGE: THE AVERAGE ENTREPRENEUR WILL FAIL

Unfortunately, according to Forbes, "8 out of 10 entrepreneurs who start businesses fail within the first 18 months." Most of these failures are caused by either their inability to sell something or their inability to account for anything.

http://www.forbes.com/sites/ericwagner/2013/09/12/five-reasons-8-out-of-10-businesses-fail/#1ebcf5bb5e3c

# THE EXCITING HISTORY OF TAXATION IN OUR COUNTRY

1862 - President Abraham Lincoln withheld taxes for the purpose of financing the civil war.

1872 - Tax withholding was abolished and the income tax was abolished totally.

1913 - Income Tax became permanent.

1917 - Withholding laws were repealed because it made employers the tax collectors.

1935 - Social security taxes were withheld by employees.

1943 - The tax withholding system was developed by famous economist Milton Friedman and others.

The amount of income tax that is withheld is determined by how an employee fills out their IRS form W4.

Well over half of the entrepreneurs that we have coached over the past decade have no clue what they are doing with their accounting, so they are behind on their taxes, their collections, payroll, and bills and it's not good. However, the good news is that we can teach you how to get your systems in order. In fact, we worked with one cosmetic surgeon who had over half a million dollars owed to him and a basketball coach who was being stolen from every month by his office manager without even knowing until business systems were put in place that revealed these facts.

HEY DARRELL, YOUR MONEY MACHINE MIGHT BE LOSING MONEY ...?

NOPE, LET'S JUST GO FASTER!

RUSH TO REVENUE
Money Cures All Problems

One of the former leading consultants for Kleiner Perkins, the venture capital fund that has funded Google, Square, and Uber once said, "I have learned from both my own successes and failures and those of many others that it's the boring stuff that matters the most. Startup success is not a consequence of good genes or being in the right place at the right time. Startup success can be engineered by following the right process, which means it can be learned, which means it can be taught."

Once we help you build a repeatable system for managing and executing the boring stuff in business, you'll be off to the races with the peace of mind knowing where you are at all times.

## BECOME AN AUTOMATIC MILLIONAIRE

Automate your savings and you will win: If you decide to invest $200 per week every two weeks for the next thirty five years you are on the planet and you earned an annual return of just 10% you find yourself as the proud owner of an account worth **$1,678,293.78**

# 5 FINANCIAL SUPER MOVES

1. Schedule and block the weekly time in your schedule when you will sit down and look at your finances.

2. Schedule where you will sit down and look at your finances.

3. Schedule and block the weekly time into your schedule to meet with your bookkeeper.

4. Schedule and block the monthly time into your schedule to meet with your accountant.

5. Work with your coach to develop an accurate pro-forma, so that you know how much money you are going to make per customer, how many customers you need to break-even per month, and how many customers you need to achieve your financial goals.

## FUN FACTS ABOUT THE AMERICAN ECONOMIC SYSTEM:

Since August 15th, 1971 the currency is no longer backed or supported by the gold standard. We now have a fiat currency. The word "fiat" is latin for "Decree or Let it be"

In November 1910 the Federal Reserve concept was created. The Federal Reserve was officially created by the 1913 Federal Reserve Act to inspire confidence in the banking system by people like you and me.

Government can now spend unlimited amounts of money by devaluing the value of your money. As an example $27,000 in 1970 would be worth $168,985.90. Data.bls.gov

# CALCULATE THE IDEAL PRICING FOR YOUR PRODUCT OR SERVICE

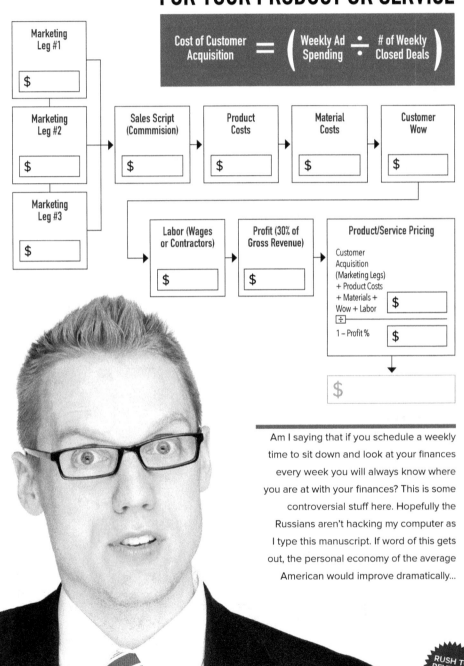

$$\text{Cost of Customer Acquisition} = \left( \text{Weekly Ad Spending} \div \text{\# of Weekly Closed Deals} \right)$$

**Marketing Leg #1** — $

**Marketing Leg #2** — $

**Marketing Leg #3** — $

**Sales Script (Commmision)** — $

**Product Costs** — $

**Material Costs** — $

**Customer Wow** — $

**Labor (Wages or Contractors)** — $

**Profit (30% of Gross Revenue)** — $

**Product/Service Pricing**

Customer Acquisition (Marketing Legs) + Product Costs + Materials + Wow + Labor — $

÷

1 – Profit % — $

$

Am I saying that if you schedule a weekly time to sit down and look at your finances every week you will always know where you are at with your finances? This is some controversial stuff here. Hopefully the Russians aren't hacking my computer as I type this manuscript. If word of this gets out, the personal economy of the average American would improve dramatically...

RUSH TO REVENUE
Money Cures All Problems

# THIS IS YOUR TIME TO THRIVE

"Vision without execution is hallucination."
**THOMAS EDISON**

"Action is the real measure of intelligence."
**NAPOLEON HILL**

"You can't build a reputation on what you are going to do."
**HENRY FORD**

"The way to get started is to quit talking and begin doing."
**WALT DISNEY**

"Quit being an intender and a pretender. Automate your savings today or retire as an overworked and broke human."
**CLAY CLARK**

"Historically it has been challenging to find someday on a standard calendar."

**CLAY CLARK**
*The founder of multiple businesses who never waited for "someday" to come*

"One way to get priorities accomplished is to schedule them on your calendar."

**LEE COCKERELL**
*Former executive president of Walt Disney World and Thrive15.com partner*

RUSH TO REVENUE
Money Cures All Problems

# STEP 14

## WHAT IS THE POINT OF ACHIEVING FINANCIAL SUCCESS?

After YOU have diligently implemented the previous proven 13 steps you will find that YOU have achieved financial success by the world's standards. Success stories like Aaron Antis growing ShawHomes.com from $24 million per year to $17 per month in sales abound within my client roster. Once you have sacrificed and made the tradeoffs needed to achieve massive success you too will become financially successful just like Josh Wilson with LivingWaterIrrigationOK.com, Randy Antrikin of PMHOKC.com, Jonathan Barnett with OXIFresh.com, Ryan and Rachel Wimpey with TipTopK9.com, etc. However, what is the point of financial success? What is the point of earning additional money?

"Having the basics—a good bed to sleep in, good relationships, good food, and good sex—is most important, and those things don't get much better when you have a lot of money or much worse when you have less."

**RAY DALIO**
*Best selling author*

During the year 2019, our clients grew at a rate of 104%. Why? Because I am focused on results and how you are going to feel when you achieve your goals and not how you feel as you are pushing through the pain needed to execute the plan and to experience real gains.

https://www.thrivetimeshow.com/testimonials/

### FACT: 96% OF BUSINESSES FAIL.

https://www.inc.com/bill-carmody/why-96-of-businesses-fail-within-10-years.html

### FACT: OUR CLIENTS GROW ON AVERAGE 104% PER YEAR AND ABOVE.

(It is harder to grow at a large percentage as the size of a company increases)

### The Shaw Homes Case Study: From $24 Million to $81 in Annual Revenue:

Aaron Antis - As 2015 drew to a close I was not sure where to go as a company to move us past the $24 million in revenue to the place where my drive and ambition wanted us to go. I had sold over $700 million in real estate personally but I couldn't figure out how to get the rest of my team to have the same drive and ambition to go higher than where they were. As we came into 2016, Steve Currington, a mortgage rep I knew in Tulsa introduced me to Clay Clark and we apprehensively signed up for a coaching service we could cancel anytime. I thought, I'll give this guy a few months to see if he actually can live up to the hype. I felt that I knew everything there was to know about sales and marketing and management but maybe he could teach me a couple new things.

Little did I know that we would go from $24 million in 2015 to $49 million in 2016, more than doubling our previous years production. Our proven systems worked in spades to spur incredible growth in leads and conversion rates through scalable systems and processes. 2017 brought growing pains from the massive growth of 2016 and Clay masterfully and patiently helped me navigate through the discovery

RUSH TO REVENUE
Money Cures All Problems

that I had to grow and change in order for the company to continue growing. Clay's message to me remained consistent as he waited to see if I would continue to heed his advice.

Every year we have worked with Clay we have broken records and 2019 we did $80 million in sales. So far in 2020 we are a pace for $122 million in sales and breaking monthly sales records each month. Clay has been an inspiration to me as a leader, a lightning rod to our sales efforts and guide post for how to manage a growing company.

Lastly I have referred many business owner friends of mine to Clay that are all thriving and growing as well. With Clay being a former DJ I believe his microphone and platform to speak life into other people's businesses needs to continue to increase. He helps people, and I would love to see him help more people. If you have any suggestions please call me and I would be glad to talk.

Aaron Antis
www.ShawHomes.com
918.645.4441
Aantis@shawhomes.com
Industry - Home Builder

A Better Sewer
Jeff Watson
www.ABetterPlumberCo.com
2018 - 2019 Up 79%
Industry - Plumber

Accolade Exteriors
Stuart Weikel
www.AccoladeExteriors.com
2018 - 2019 Up 82%
Industry - Window Replacement

Amy Baltimore, CPA
Amy Baltimore
www.AmyBaltimoreCPA.com
2018 - 2019 Up 34%
Industry - Accountant

Angel's Touch
Christina Nemes
www.CapeCodAutoBodyandDetailing.com
2018 - $988,241.28
2019 - $1,646,327.37
Growth - 67%
Industry - Auto Body and Restoration Shop

Back to Basics Builders
Joe Burbey
www.HomeRemodelingMilwaukee.com
2018 - 2019 Up 35%
Industry - Home Remodeling

RUSH TO REVENUE
Money Cures All Problems

Barbee Cookies
Kat Graham
www.BarbeeCookies.com
2014 - 2015 Up 140%
Industry - Bakery

Best Buy Window Treatment
Ergun Aral
www.BestBuyWindowTreatments.com
2018 - 2019 Up 76%
Industry - Window Treatments

Bigfoot Restoration
Marc Lucero & Stephen Small
www.BigFootRestoration.com
2018 - 2019 Up 112%
Industry - Disaster
Restoration and Repair

Bogard and Sons Construction
Andy Bogard
www.BogardandSons.com
2018 - 2019 Up 32%
Industry - Home Building
and Remodeling

Breakout Creative
Chris De Jesus
www.BreakOutCreativeCompany.com
Up 59% Total
Industry - Advertising

Brian T. Armstrong
Construction Incorporated
Brian T. Armstrong

www.BrianTArmstrongConstructionInc.com
2017 - 2018 Up 29%
2018 - 2019 Up 89%
Industry - Home Builder

C&R Contracting
Ryan Kilday
www.ColoradoContracting.com
2018 - 2019 Up 240%
Industry - Contracting and Remodeling

Catalyst Communication
Adam Duran
www.
CatalystCommunicationsGroupInc.com
2018 - 2019 Up 44%
Industry - Commercial Security Systems

Chaney Construction
Jim and Amy Chaney
www.ChaneyConstructionTX.com
2018 - 2019 Up 19%
Industry - Home Builder

Citywide Mechanical
Terrance Thomas
www.CityWide-Mechanical.com
2018 - 2019 Up 118%
Industry - Heating and Air

CK Electric
Chad Kudlacek
www.CKElectricOmaha.com
2018 - 2019 Up 25%
Industry - Electrician

Colaw Fitness
Charles and Amber Colaw
www.ColawFitness.com
2018 - 2019 Up 15%
Industry - Fitness Gym

Compass Roofing
Robert Alsbrooks & Sonny Ordonez
www.CompassRoofing.com
2018 - 2019 Up 103%
Industry - Commercial and
Residential Roofing

Complete Carpet
Nathan & Toni Sevrinus
www.CompleteCarpetTulsa.com
2017 - 2019 Up 298%
Industry - Carpet Cleaning

Comfort Pro
Steve Bagwell
www.ComfortPro-Inc.com
2018 - 2019 Up 28%
Industry - Heating and Air

CT Tech
Christopher Tracy
https://cttec.net/
2018 - 2019 Up 77%
Industry - IT Support

Curtis Music
Ron Curtis
www.CurtisMusicAcademy.com
2018 - 2019 Up 58%
Industry - Music Teacher

Custom Automation
Technologies Incorporated
Dan Hoehnen
www.CustomAutomationTech.com
2018 - 2019 Up 16%
Industry - Custom Automation

D&D Custom Homes
Dave Tucker
www.MidSouthHomeBuilder.com
2018 - 2019 Up 45%
Industry - Custom Home Builder

Da Vinci
Josh Fellman and Jerome Garrett
www.500KMSP.com
2018 - 2019 Up 1,097%
Managed Service Provider Consulting

Danco
Denise Richter
www.DancoPump.com
2018 - 2019 Up 17%
Industry - manufacturing
and distribution

Delricht Research
Tyler and Rachel Hastings
www.DelrichtResearch.com
2018 - 2019 Up 300%
Industry - Clinical Research

Dr. Breck Kasbaum Chiropractor
Dr. Breck Kasbaum
www.DrBreck.com
2018 - 2019 Up 50%
Industry - Chiropractic

Duct Armor
Tim Borgne
https://www.ductarmor.com/
2015 - 2016 Up 20%
Industry - Air Duct Repair

Dynamic Electrical So
Edward Durant
www.DynaElec.com
2018 - 2019 Up 16%
Industry - Electrician

ECS Electric
James Crews
www.ECSElectricllc.com
2018 - 2019 Up 26%
Industry - Electrician

Edmond Dental
Dr. Joseph Tucker
www.EdmondDentalatDeerCreek.com
2018 - 2019 Up 205%
Industry - Dentist

Electrical Investments
James Henry
www.ElectricalInvestments.com
2018 - 2019 Up 21%
Industry - Electrician

EnviZion Insurance
Austin Grieci
www.EZInsurancePlan.com
2018 - 2019 Up 800%
Industry - Auto Insurance

Full Package Media
Thomas James Crosson
www.FullPackageMedia.com
2018 - 2019 Up 15%
Commercial Real Estate Photography

Gable's Excavating Incorporated
Levi Gable
www.GEI-USA.com
2018 - 2019 Up 66%
Industry - Utility Contractor

The Garage
Roy Coggeshall
www.TheGarageBA.com
2018 - 2019 Up 19%
2017 - Present Up 70%
Industry - Auto Repair

The Grill Gun
Bob Healey
www.GrillBlazer.com
From Idea to Manufactured Product
8,725 Funders
Raised $920,009.00 Crowd
Funding the Invention
Industry - Retail Products

H2Oasis Float Center
Debra Worthington
www.H2OasisFloatCenter.com
Up 17% Total
Industry - Float Therapy

Handy Bros Services
David Visser
www.HandyBros-Services.com
2018 - 2019 Up 136%
Industry - Handyman

HealthRide
Ryan Graff
www.HealthRideTulsa.org
2018 - 2019 Up 10%
Industry - Non-Emergency
Medical Transportation

Healthworks Chiropractic
Jay Schroeder
www.HealthworksChiropractic.net
2018 - 2019 Up 24%
Industry - Chiropractic
Hood and Associates CPA's, PC

Paul Hood
www.HoodCPAs.com
2018 - 2019 Up 61%
Industry - Accountant

The Hub Gym
Luke Owens
www.TheHubGym.com
2018 - 2019 Up 66.38%
Industry - Fitness Gym

Impressions Painting
Manuel Mora
www.ImpressionsPaintingTulsa.com
2018 - 2019 Up 41%
Industry - House Painting

Inspired Spaces
Josh Fellman and Jerome Garrett
www.InspiredSpacesOK.com
2018 - 2019 Up 40%
Industry - Epoxy Flooring

Jameson Fine Cabinetry
Jamie Fagel
www.JamesonFineCabinetry.com
2018 - 2019 Up 31%
Industry - Home Improvement

Jean Briese
Jean Briese
www.JeanBriese.com
2018 - 2019 Up 90%
4. Motivational Speaker

KAE Edward Plumbing
Ron & Jacqueline Mader
www.KaeEdwardPlumbing.com
2018 - 2019 Up 46%
Industry - Plumber

Kelly Construction Group
Jon Kelly
www.KellyConstructionGroup.com
2018 - 2019 Up 42%
Industry - General Contractor

Kona Honu
Byron Kay
www.KonaHonuDivers.com
2018 - 2019 Up 14%
Industry - Diving Tours and
Scuba Instruction

Kurb to Kitchen
Lonny & Rinda Myers
www.KurbtoKitchenLLC.com
2018 - 2019 Up 126%
Industry - Home Remodeling

Kvell Fitness & Nutrition
Brett Denton
www.KvellFit.com
2018-2019 Up 35%+
Industry - Fitness Gym

Lake Martin Mini Mall
Jason Lett
www.LakeMartinCubed.com
2018 - $685,804.00
2019 - $782,551.00
14% Growth
Industry - Retail Products

Lakeshore Plumbing
Mike Boulte
www.LakeShorePlumbingOKC.com
2018 - 2019 Up 100%
Industry - Plumber

Laundry Barn
Josh Fellman
www.TheLaundryBarn.com
2018 - 2019 Up 100%
Industry - Laundromat

Living Water Irrigation
Josh Wilson
www.LivingWaterIrrigationOK.com
2017 - 2019 Up 600%
Industry - Sprinkler Install

Mennis Heating
Mike Ennis
www.MennisHeatingandCooling.com
2018 - 2019 Up 400%
Industry - Heating and Air

Metal Roof Contractors
Doug Yarholar
www.MetalRoofContractorsOK.com
2018 - 2019 Up 14%
Industry - Metal Roof Contractor

Mod Scenes
Steven Hall
www.ModScenes.com
2018 - 2019 Up 83%
Industry - Stage Design

Morrow, Lai and Kitterman
Pediatric Dentistry
Dr. Mark Morrow, Dr. April Lai,
and Dr. Kerry Kitterman
www.MLKDentistry.com
2018 - 2019 Up 42%
Industry - Dentist

Mr. Rooter
Joshua Creasy
www.MrRooter.com/New-Braunfels/
2018 - 2019 Up 75%
Industry - Plumber

Multi-Clean
Kevin Thomas
www.MultiCleanOK.com
2018 - 2019 Up 14%
Industry - Commercial Cleaning

OK Roof Nerds
Marty Grisham
www.OKRoofNerds.com
2018 - 2019 Up 74%
Industry - Commercial and
Residential Roofer

One Way Plumbing
Chad Ward
www.OneWayPlumbing.biz
2018 - 2019 Up 11%
Industry - Plumbing

Oxi Fresh
Jonathan Barnett
Matt Kline - Franchise Developer
www.OxiFresh.com
2007 to 2019 - 400 Locations Opened
Industry - Carpet Cleaning

Pappagallo's Pizza
Dave Rich
www.Pappagallos.com
2018 - 2019 Up 21%
Industry - Restaurant

Platinum Pest
Jennifer and Jared Johnson
www.PlatinumPestandLawn.com
2018-2019 - 25% Growth
2017-2018 - 43% Growth
Industry - Pest Control

PMH OKC
Randy Antrikan
www.PMHOKC.com
2018 - 2019 Up 70%
Industry - Outdoor Living
/ Retail Products

Precision Calibration
Nathan Saylor
www.PrecisionCalibrations.com
2018 - 2019 Up 62%
Industry - Equipment Calibration

Quality Surfaces
John Cook
www.QualitySurfacesIn.com
2018 - 2019 Up 84%
Industry - Commercial and
Residential Remodeling

RC Auto Specialists
Roy Coggeshall
www.RCAutoSpecialists.com
2018 - 2019 Up 9%
Industry - Auto Repair

Rescue Roofer TX
Wesley Cannon
www.RoofingDenton.com
2018 - 2019 Up 79%
Industry - Commercial and
Residential Roofer

Revitalize Medical Spa
Lindsey Blankenship and Crista Hobbs
www.RevitalizeMedicalSpa.com
2018 - 2019 Up 36%
Industry - Medical Cosmetics

Roofing & Siding Smiths
Zach Potts
www.RoofingandSidingSmiths.com
2018 - 2019 Up 67%
Industry - Roofing and Siding

Rogers Plumbing
Roger Patterson
https://plumberinaustin.com
2018 - 2019 Up 33%
Industry - Plumber

Scotch Construction
Tim Scotch
www.ScotchConstruction.com
2017 - 2019 Up 492%
Industry - Home Builder

Shaw Homes
Aaron Antis
www.ShawHomes.com
2018 - 2019 Up 116%
Industry - Custom Home Builder

Sierra Pools
Cody Albright
www.SierraPoolsandSpas.com
2017 - 2019 Up 309%
Industry - Pool Construction

Snow Bear Air
Daniel Ramos
www.SnowBearAir.com
2018 - 2019 Up 41%
Industry - Heating and Air

Southeastern Computer Associates
Ben Miner
https://sca-atl.com/
2018 - $2,011,394.51 -
2019 - $5,531,144.01
Industry - IT Support

Spot-On Plumbing
Brandon Brown
www.SpotOnPlumbingTulsa.com
2018 - 2019 Up 120%
Industry - Plumber

Spurrell & Associates Chartered
Professional Accountants
Josh Spurrell
www.Spurrell.ca
2018 - 2019 Up 50%
Industry - Accounting

Struct Construction
Brandon Haaga
www.StructConstruction.com
2018 - 2019 Up 60%
Industry - Construction Contractor

Tesla Electric
Felix Keil
www.TeslaElectricColorado.com
2018 - 2019 Up 60%
Industry - Tesla Electric

Tip Top K9
Ryan and Rachel Wimpey
www.TipTopK9.com
1 Location - 10 Locations
Industry - Dog Training

Trinity Employment
Cory Minter
www.TrinityEmployment.com
2018-2019 Up 35%
Industry - Staffing

Turley Solutions & Innovations
Rance Turley
www.TSI.lc
2018 - 2019 Up 300%
Industry - IT Support

Tuscaloosa Ophthalmology
Doctor Timothy Johnson
www.TTownEyes.com
2018 - 2019  Up 16%
Industry - Doctor

Viva Med
Chris Lacroix
www.MyVivaMed.com
2018 - 2019 Up 90%
Industry - Primary Care Physicians

Veteran Home Exterior
James Peterson
www.VeteranHomeExterior.com
2018 - 2019 Up 145%
Industry - Window Replacement

White Glove Auto
Myron Kirkpatrick
WhiteGloveAutoTulsa.com
2018 - 2019 - 27%
Industry - Auto Detailing

Williams Contracting
Travis Williams
www.Will-Con.com
2018 - 2019 Up 33%
Industry - Construction Management

Witness Security
Keith Schultz
www.WitnessLLC.com
2017 - 2019 Up 300%
Industry - Home Security Systems

### Money Is Simply a Magnifier (Both Good and Bad):

Money is just a magnifier, and I have consistently found that teaching YOU how to make more money and how to create both time and financial freedom simply allows YOU to become more of who YOU are, both GOOD and BAD.

If you are generous, having increased financial means will allow you to give even more to help those in need. If you like going out to eat, with additional income you will have the financial resources to NOW go out to eat more often. If you love traveling, with financial abundance in your wallet, you will be able to travel even more. With additional cash in the bank, if you are excited about buying exotic cars, having increased financial resources will allow you to buy even more exotic cars because money is just a magnifier. However, it is my sincere and highest desire that I haven't taught you the proven processes and success strategies so that you can become a MASSIVE ASS because the world already has enough of those (Mark Zuckerberg, Jack Dorsey, Bill Gates, etc.)

"[36] For what shall it profit a man, if he shall gain the whole world, and lose his own soul?"

**MARK 8:36**
*KJV*

So as we complete this workbook (and potentially this workshop) together, I would encourage you to sit down with yourself, with your spouse and with GOD'S PLAN FOR YOUR LIFE firmly placed in your mind and I would ask yourself the following question.

If you had all of the money in the world what goals would you have for your faith, family, finances, fitness, friendship and fun.

I would encourage you to take 30 minute to actually sketch out your ideal calendar in a perfect world where you have the financial freedom and time freedom needed to dictate what you will do with your days and whom you will spend your time with. Don't mail it in here. This is the entire point of learning how to grow a successful business. Fill in the calendar below the time that you will devote to your faith, your family, your finances, your fitness, your friend and your pursuit of fun. Don't be afraid to schedule guitar lessons, workouts, time to take your kids camping or that all important trip that you've been putting off. Every day that we are given on this planet is a gift from our God above, however what we do with each and every day is our gift to God. Remember being present is a present. But, remember, only what gets scheduled gets done.

225

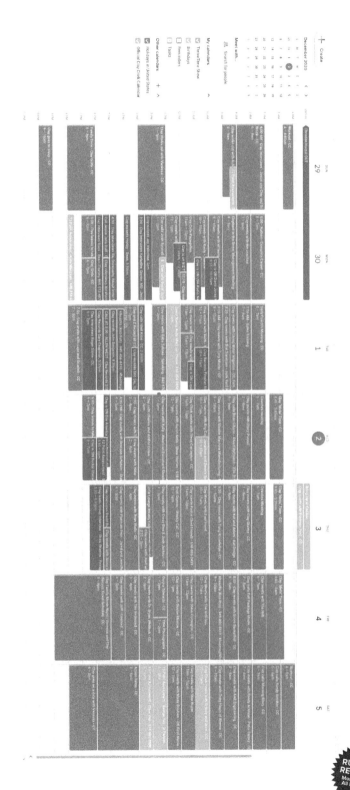

RUSH TO
REVENUE
Money Cures
All Problems

# CHAPTER 17

# YOU HAVE WHAT IT TAKES

## A LITTLE ENCOURAGEMENT FOR YOU

> "An educated man is not, necessarily, one who has an abundance of general or specialized knowledge. An educated man is one who has so developed the faculties of his mind that he may acquire anything he wants, or its equivalent, without violating the rights of others."

**NAPOLEAN HILL**
*The Best-selling self-help author of all time and the former apprentice of andrew carnegie.*

Doctor Z and I know that you have what it takes to become successful and you know that you have what it takes too or you wouldn't be reading this book. My friend, exposing yourself to this practical business training is the first step, but now you must begin executing and turning your dreams into reality by becoming a pig-headed diligent doer who won't stop until you get to that time freedom and financial freedom that you are chasing. Don't get distracted by the world around you and be sucked into this false belief that now is not the time and that someday things will be better. We all have only 24 hours per day and 7 days per week to work with and last time I checked, "someday" was not one of the days of the week. To build your faith, I've done the research and created a list of 73 famous entrepreneurs who went on to achieve massive success without a college degree. Whether you have formal education or not, you can achieve success. And this is your year to THRIVE!!!!!

## FUN FACT

The following entrepreneurs and world-leaders struggled through life because they didn't have a degree from a fancy business college (forgive the sarcasm spasms):

### Abraham Lincoln

Despite not having earned the respect of his peers by obtaining a college degree, he went on to become a lawyer and president of the United States. Because he chose to be self-taught, he never did stop learning until the day of his death.

1832 - Lost job and was defeated for state legislature.

1833 - Failed in business.

1843 - Lost his attempt to be nominated for Congress.

1848 - Lost renomination for Congress.

1849 - Rejected in his attempt to become land officer.

1854 - Defeated for U.S. Senate.

1856 - Defeated for nomination for Vice President.

1848 - Defeated for U.S. Senate.

### Amadeo Peter Giannini

Despite not knowing what he was doing because he didn't have a master's degree from a fancy business college, he went on to become the multi-millionaire founder of Bank of America after dropping out of high school.

### Andrew Carnegie

Despite being an elementary school dropout, this man went on to become the world's wealthiest man during his lifetime. Amazing, since he couldn't possibly have known what he was doing because he didn't have a college degree.

### Andrew Jackson

This guy went on to become an attorney, a U.S. president, a general, a judge, and a congressman despite being home-schooled and having no formal education at all.

### Anne Beiler

The "Princess of Pretzels" went on to start Auntie Anne's Pretzels and to become a millionaire, despite having dropped out of high school. I bet she's disappointed she missed out on the once-in-a-lifetime experiences that so many college graduates with $100,000 of debt enjoyed.

### Ansel Adams

I don't know if you are into world-famous photographers or not, but if you are, you know that Ansel Adams became arguably the best photographer in the world despite not graduating from a college of liberal arts. I wonder how he even knew to take the lens cap off of his camera without a college degree.

### Barry Diller

This dude may be a billionaire and Hollywood mogul who founded Fox Broadcasting Company, but I am not impressed with him because he does not have a college degree.

### Benjamin Franklin

This guy might have invented the Franklin stove, lightning rods, bifocals, and other assorted inventions while working as a founding father of the United States, but I can tell you that he had a hole in his soul where his degree should have been.

### Billy Joe (Red) McCombs

Red became a billionaire, but did he have a degree? No. And that is exactly why he doesn't get invited to any of those fancy alumni gatherings, which he would be too busy to attend anyway because he's off counting his money. Seriously, if he started counting the billions of dollars he made by founding Clear Channel media, he would never finish.

### Coco Chanel

She may have a perfume that bears her name, but I am not impressed with her because she doesn't have a degree.

### Colonel Harlan Sanders

This guy dropped out of elementary school and all he knew about was chicken. Sure he made millions, but I didn't truly have respect for him until he finally earned that law degree by correspondence.

### Dave Thomas

Every time I pull into Wendy's to enjoy a delicious snack wrap, I find myself thinking about what a complete waste of talent Dave was. He could have had trillions of dollars if only he had earned a degree.

### David Geffen

Like a true loser, he dropped out of college after completing only one year. My, his parents must be disappointed. I feel bad just writing about this billionaire founder of Geffen Records and co-founder of DreamWorks.

### David Green

David, oh David. I bet you feel bad about your billions and spend everyday living in regret because you do not have a college degree. I know that you took $600 and famously turned that into billions as the founder of Hobby Lobby, but you could have been a good attorney or a bureaucrat or a politician we all could watch argue to an empty room on C-SPAN.

### David Karp

This guy's last name should be carp, because this bottom feeder obviously will never amount to anything – well, except being the multi-millionaire founder of Tumblr. If he hadn't dropped out of school at age 15, I would respect him more.

### David Neeleman

This guy started a little airline (JetBlue) to compensate for his lack of a degree. I don't even feel safe on the world's most profitable airline because its founder doesn't have a degree.

### David Oreck

David Oreck truly had a career that sucked. This college dropout and multi-millionaire founder of the Oreck vacuum company created vacuums that have sucked the dirt out of carpets for years.

### Debbi Fields

Oh, so sad. Little Debbie, the founder Mrs. Fields Chocolate Chippery, never knew the pride that one could feel upon earning a college degree.

### DeWitt Wallace

DeWitt may have founded Reader's Digest, but I'm sure that he could not truly enjoy reading in an intelligent way because he never earned his college degree.

---

## EDITOR'S NOTE: It took Clay three weeks to alphabetize this list of college dropouts because he doesn't have a degree.

---

### Dustin Moskovitz

Dustin is credited as being one of the founders of that little company called Facebook that only moms, dads, cousins, kids, adults, and humans use. I bet he wishes he had stayed in school at Harvard.

### Frank Lloyd Wright

Frank may have become the most famous architect of all time, but I cannot respect a man who never attended high school.

### Frederick Henry Royce

Okay, so a Rolls-Royce is a symbol of automotive excellence for many people, but this guy had to have been compensating for the fact that he knew nothing about anything because he was an elementary school dropout.

### George Eastman

Perhaps you are not old enough to know about the Kodak brand that used to control the world as part of the Illuminati. How George founded this little company despite dropping out of high school is beyond me. It's so sad.

### H. Wayne Huizenga

Wayne is a beautiful man and founder of WMX Garbage Company, and he also helped launch the Blockbuster Video chain. Good for him! Because without a degree, he was basically screwed.

### Henry Ford

Okay, so I've mentioned this guy in the book, but without a college degree, you can bet this billionaire founder of the Ford Motor Company was never respected by his father-in-law.

### Henry J. Kaiser

This multimillionaire and founder of Kaiser Aluminum didn't even graduate from high school. Think about it. Without a diploma, there was no way he could have become one of those pharmaceutical reps who delivers sales presentations and catering to doctors every day in exchange for their allegiance in writing prescriptions for the drugs the rep is peddling.

### Hyman Golden

This guy spent his whole life making drinks and millions. I bet you the founder of Snapple lived a life of regret while endlessly chanting to himself, "Why me? No Degree. Why me? No degree."

### Ingvar Kamprad

I believe IKEA's business model is in jeopardy. Their founder has no degree. The lines of customers are now so long that no one even wants to go there anymore. Oh...and he's dyslexic.

### Isaac Merrit Singer

This sewing machine inventor dropped out of high school because he was spending all his time sewing. I am SEW sorry for him.

### Jack Crawford Taylor

Although this man did serve honorably as a World War II fighter pilot for the Navy, I wonder what he is going to fall back on if his Enterprise Rent-a-Car venture fails.

### James Cameron

Avatar...overrated. Titanic...overrated. Winning an Oscar... overrated. But what did you expect from a director, writer, and film guy who dropped out of college?

### Jay Van Andel

A billionaire co-founder of Amway...not impressive without a degree. He does not know the meaning of life.

### Jerry Yang

Who even uses Yahoo anyway, other than the 20% of the world that does? This guy threw it all away and dropped out of a PhD program. I bet you he can't even spell "Yahoo!"

### Jimmy Dean

Food is so simple. You grow it. You eat it. You raise it. You kill it and eat it. How complex could it be if a man was able to start this multi-million dollar company after dropping out of high school at age 16?

### Jimmy Iovine

This man grew up as the son of a secretary and a longshoreman. However, at the age of 19 his ambition had become his mission. Obsessed with making records, he began working as a studio professional around the year of 1972 when a friend of his got him a job cleaning a recording studio. Soon he found himself recording with John Lennon, Bruce Springsteen and other top artists. In 1973 he landed a full-time job on the staff of the New York recording studio, Record Plant where he worked on Meat Loaf's *Bat Out of Hell* album and Springsteen's *Born to Run* album. He went on to be involved in the production of more than 250 million albums. In 2006, Iovine teamed with Dr. Dre to found Beats Electronics. This company was purchased by Apple for $3 billion in May 2014. I hope he goes on to be successful despite not having a degree.

### John Mackey

The guy who founded Whole Foods Market, the millennial mecca of the great organic panic that has swept our nation, enrolled and dropped out of college six times. Now he's stuck working at a grocery store in a dead-end job.

### John Paul DeJoria

This man is the billionaire co-founder of John Paul Mitchell Systems and dude who also founded Patron Spirits. That's it. That's all he's accomplished. No degree.

### Joyce C. Hall

This guy spent his whole life writing apology cards to his family for shaming them by not graduating from college. When he wasn't doing that, he was running that little company he founded called Hallmark.

### Kemmons Wilson

This dude started the Holiday Inn chain after dropping out of high school. But then what? What's he doing now? Well he's not buying huge amounts of college logo apparel and running down to the college football stadium eight Saturdays per year while talking about the good old days with his frat brothers because he doesn't have a degree.

### Kevin Rose

This dude dropped out of college and started a company called Digg.com. I'm not impressed with his millions. I just want to see that degree.

### Kirk Kerkorian

I did see a Boyz II Men concert at the Mirage Resorts that this guy owns. But, I have never stayed at the Mandalay Bay resort that he owns in Las Vegas more than once. It's good that he owns MGM Studios because the closest he'll ever come to a degree is if he makes a movie about himself getting a degree. He dropped out of school in 8th grade.

### Larry Ellison

Larry is the billionaire co-founder of Oracle software company and he is a man who dropped out of two different colleges. Oh, the regret he must feel.

### Leandro Rizzuto

This guy spent his time building Conair and that was it. Now, just because he is billionaire, does he think we should respect him even though he does not have a degree?

### Leslie Wexner

My wife buys stuff from the L Brands (the global retail empire that owns Victoria's Secret, Bath & Body Works, and Limited), but I am still not impressed with the fact that this law school dropout started a billion-dollar brand with $5,000.

### Mark Ecko

If you are one of those people who has success based upon the success you have, then I suppose Mark Ecko is impressive. This multi-millionaire is the founder of Mark Ecko Enterprises, but he dropped out of college.

### Mary Kay Ash

I feel like Prince should have written a song about the pink Cadillacs that Mary Kay was famous for giving to her top sales reps. But I am not impressed with her because she didn't attend college.

### Michael Dell

He may be the billionaire founder of Dell Computers, but he probably doesn't feel like a billionaire since he never experienced the college joys of drunken music festivals and regrettable one-night stands.

### Milton Hershey

Like I always say, "If you drop out of 4th grade you are going to spend your entire life making chocolate." That is what the founder of Hershey's Milk Chocolate did.

### Rachael Ray

Her happiness and genuine love for people and food makes me mad because without formal culinary arts training, this Food Network cooking show star and food industry entrepreneur is just a sham.

### Ray Kroc

He dropped out of high school, founded McDonald's, and spent his whole life saying, "Do you want fries with that?" So sad.

### Richard Branson

So he's the billionaire founder of Virgin Records, Virgin Atlantic Airways, Virgin Mobile, and more. But did he graduate from high school? No. He dropped out of his high school at the age of 16. So sad.

### Richard Schulze

He's the Best Buy founder, but he did not attend college. Doesn't he know that the investment in a college degree is truly the Best Buy you can ever make?

### Rob Kalin

Rob is the founder of Etsy, but who even uses Etsy other than all of the humans on earth? This dude flunked out of high school, then he enrolled in art school. He created a fake student ID for MIT so he could take the courses that he wanted. His professors were so impressed by his scam that they actually helped him get into NYU. Rob, you have to get it together.

### Ron Popeil

The dude who is constantly talking about dehydrating your meat and the multimillionaire founder of Ronco did not graduate from college.

### Rush Limbaugh

This guy irritates half of America every day for three hours per day. I believe that this multi-millionaire media maven and radio talk show host would be more liked if he had graduated from a liberal arts college and would have purchased a Prius pre-loaded with left-wing bumper stickers.

### Russell Simmons

This guy is co-founder of Def Jam records and the founder of the Russell Simmons Music Group. He's also the founder of Phat Farm fashions and a bestselling author. He didn't graduate from college because he claims to have been too busy introducing rap and hip hop music to the planet.

### S. Daniel Abraham

This man founded Slim-Fast without even having a degree in nutrition. Outside of the millions of people who use his products every day to lose weight, who is going to trust him with their health since he doesn't even have a college degree?

### Sean John Combs

The man who is en route to becoming the first hip-hop billionaire in part because of his ownership in the Ciroc Vodka brand did not graduate from college because he was spending his time discovering and promoting Mary J. Blige, The Notorious B.I.G., Jodeci, and other R&B stars. If this man ever wants to become truly successful, he will go back to Howard University and get that degree.

### Shawn Fanning

This is the music industry-killing devil who created Napster and went on to become a multi-millionaire. If he would have stayed in college, he would have learned to follow the rules.

### Simon Cowell

This famous TV producer, judger of people, American Idol, The X Factor, and Britain's Got Talent star dropped out of high school. He has been negative ever since. He obviously needs a college degree to calm him down because I've never met a college graduate who is mean.

### Steve Jobs

This hippie dropped out of college and frankly, his little Apple company barely made it.

### Steve Madden

Steve dropped out of college and now spends his entire life making shoes. He may be worth millions, but I'm sure that you and I are not impressed.

### Steve Wozniak

Okay, so I did know that Steve Jobs co-founded Apple with this guy and both of them became billionaires, but they experienced what I call a "hollow success" because they did not take the time to earn a college degree.

### Theodore Waitt

This man became a billionaire by selling a PC to every human possible during the 1990s. He may have co-founded Gateway computers but without a degree, how will he ever experience true success? I bet that he regrets not having a degree.

### Thomas Edison

Tommy Boy wasn't smart enough to graduate from high school, yet he was crazy enough to invent the modern light bulb, recorded audio, and recorded video. I am never impressed with crazy people who don't graduate from high school.

### Tom Anderson

This dude co-founded MySpace after dropping out of high school. He made his millions, but who ever had a MySpace account anyway?

RUSH TO REVENUE
Money Cures All Problems

### Ty Warner

I think the only thing weirder than collecting Beanie Babies is to have invented them. To cover up this weird Beanie Babies fixation, this billionaire has gone on to purchase real estate. College would have taught him that it is not normal for an adult to be interested in stuffed animals.

### Vidal Sassoon

This dude founded Vidal Sassoon after dropping out of high school. Had he graduated from college, I'm sure his product would have been better.

### W. Clement Stone

This guy started the billion-dollar insurance company called Combined Insurance. He then went on to start *Success* Magazine and write books to keep himself busy because he felt so bad that he didn't have a college degree.

### Wally "Famous" Amos

This man did not graduate from high school and spent almost his entire working career making people fat by selling them Famous Amos cookies. If he had graduated from college, he might have invented a product that makes people thin and able to live forever while tasting good, you know, like carrots.

### Walt Disney

This struggling entrepreneur who never really figured it out co-founded the Walt Disney Company with his brother Roy. He didn't even graduate from high school, which is probably why he spent his entire life drawing cartoons.

### Wolfgang Puck

Okay, so my wife and I buy his soup. Okay, so I have eaten at his restaurant a few times. But I can't respect a man who dropped out of high school at the age of 14. Yes, he's opened up 16 restaurants and 80 bistros. So what? Respecting people like this sets a bad example for kids because not everyone can go on to become a successful entrepreneur, but everyone can incur $100,000 of student loan debt before finding a soul-sucking job doing something they don't like in exchange for a paycheck.

# MAKE THE WORLD A BETTER PLACE
Subscribe to the ThriveTime Show Podcast today at www.ThriveTimeShow.com

# ACTION ITEMS

1. Pass on what you've learned by writing a Google Review. search for "ThriveTime Show Jenks" on Google Maps and write a review today!

2. Don't miss a radio show or podcast. Subscribe on Itunes, Spotify, Stitcher or listen at ThrivetimeShow.com

3. Get all of the interactive downloadables by signing up today at ThriveTimeShow.com.

# WANT MORE?

**Check out the Ultimate Textbook for Starting, Running & Growing Your Own Business!**

### Start Here

NEVER before has entrepreneurship been delivered in an UNFILTERED, real and raw way... until now. This book is NOT for people that want a politically correct and silver-lined happy-go-lucky view of entrepreneurship. That's crap. Supported by case studies and testimonials from entrepreneurs that have grown their businesses all over the planet using these best practice systems, former U.S. Small Business Administration Entrepreneur of the Year, Clay Clark, shares the specific action steps for successful business systems, hilarious stories from situations that every entrepreneur faces, and entrepreneurship factoids that are guaranteed to blow your mind.

# Invite a Friend to Join You at the World's Best 2-Day Intensive Business Workshop

**Get specific and practical training on how to grow your business**

## www.ThriveTimeShow.com/Conference

# WANT ONE-ON-ONE MENTORSHIP AND BUSINESS COACHING? VISIT WWW.THRIVETIMESHOW.COM/COACHING

Let our team help you execute your action items and guide you down the proven path (see ThriveTimeShow.com)

# CLIENT WINS / CASE STUDIES

During the year 2019 our clients grew at a rate of 104%. Why? Because I am focused on results and how you are going to feel when you achieve your goals and not how you feel as you are pushing through the pain needed to execute the plan and to make experience real gains. https://www.thrivetimeshow.com/testimonials/

## FACT: 96% OF BUSINESSES FAIL.

*https://www.inc.com/bill-carmody/why-96-of-businesses-fail-within-10-years.html*

## FACT: OUR CLIENTS GROW ON AVERAGE 104% PER YEAR AND ABOVE. (IT IS HARDER TO GROW AT A LARGE PERCENTAGE AS THE SIZE OF A COMPANY INCREASES)

## THE SHAW HOMES CASE STUDY:
### FROM $24 MILLION TO $81 IN ANNUAL REVENUE:

Aaron Antis - As 2015 drew to a close I was not sure where to go as a company to move us past the $24 million in revenue to the place where my drive and ambition wanted us to go. I had sold over $700 million in real estate personally but I couldn't figure out how to get the rest of my team to have the same drive and ambition to go higher than where they were. As we came into 2016, Steve Currington, a mortgage rep I knew in Tulsa introduced me to Clay Clark and we apprehensively signed up for a coaching service we could cancel anytime. I thought, I'll give this guy a few months to see if he actually can live up to the hype. I felt that I knew everything there was to know about sales and marketing and management but maybe he could teach me a couple new things.

Little did I know that we would go from $24 million in 2015 to $49 million in 2016, more than doubling our previous years production. Our proven systems worked in spades to spur incredible growth in leads and conversion rates through scalable systems and processes. 2017 brought growing pains from the massive growth of 2016 and Clay masterfully and patiently helped me navigate through the discovery that I had to grow and change in order for the company to continue to grow.

Clay's message to me remained consistent as he waited to see if I would continue to heed his advice.

Every year we have worked with Clay we have broken records and 2019 we did $80 million in sales. So far in 2020 we are a pace for $122 million in sales and breaking monthly sales records each month. Clay has been an inspiration to me as a leader, a lightning rod to our sales efforts and guide post for how to manage a growing company.

Lastly I have referred many business owner friends of mine to Clay that are all thriving and growing as well. With Clay being a former DJ I believe his microphone and platform to speak life into other people's businesses needs to continue to increase. He helps people, and I would love to see him help more people. If you have any questions please call me and I would be glad to talk.

### A BETTER SEWER
- » Jeff Watson
- » www.ABetterPlumberCo.com
- » 2018 - 2019 Up 79%
- » Industry - Plumber

### AMY LYNN INTERIORS - 53%
- » Amy Kearns
- » AmyLynn-Interiors.com

### A NEW IMAGE - 26%
- » Dr. Dwight Korgan
- » 918-341-2000
- » Anewimageok.com

### ACCOLADE EXTERIORS
- » Stuart Weikel
- » www.AccoladeExteriors.com
- » 2018 - 2019 Up 82%
- » Industry - Window Replacement

### AMY BALTIMORE, CPA
- » Amy Baltimore
- » www.AmyBaltimoreCPA.com
- » 2018 - 2019 Up 34%
- » Industry - Accountant

**ANGEL'S TOUCH**

» Christina Nemes

» www.CapeCodAutoBodyandDetailing.com

» 2018 - $988,241.28

» 2019 - $1,646,327.37

» 2020 - 2021 = 26% growth

» Growth - 67%

» Industry - Auto Body and Restoration Shop

**BACK TO BASICS BUILDERS**

» Joe Burbey

» www.HomeRemodelingMilwaukee.com

» 2018 - 2019 Up 35%

» Industry - Home Remodeling

**BARBEE COOKIES**

» Kat Graham

» www.BarbeeCookies.com

» 2014 - 2015 Up 140%

» Industry - Bakery

**BEST BUY WINDOW TREATMENT**

» Ergun Aral

» www.BestBuyWindowTreatments.com

» 2018 - 2019 Up 76%

» Industry - Window Treatments

**BIGFOOT RESTORATION**

» Marc Lucero & Stephen Small

» www.BigFootRestoration.com

» 2018 - 2019 Up 112%

» Industry - Disaster Restoration and Repair

**BOGARD AND SONS CONSTRUCTION**

» Andy Bogard

» www.BogardandSons.com

» 2018 - 2019 Up 32%

» Industry - Home Building and Remodeling

### BREAKOUT CREATIVE

» Chris De Jesus
» www.BreakOutCreativeCompany.com
» Up 59% Total
» Industry - Advertising

### BRIAN T. ARMSTRONG CONSTRUCTION INCORPORATED

» Brian T. Armstrong
» www.BrianTArmstrongConstructionInc.com
» 2017 - 2018 Up 29%
» 2018 - 2019 Up 89%
» Industry - Home Builder

### CANON PUMPS - 111%

» Charlie Ulrich
» 801-582-7867
» Cannonpumps.com

### C&R CONTRACTING

» Ryan Kilday
» www.ColoradoContracting.com
» 2018 - 2019 Up 240%
» Industry - Contracting and Remodeling

### CATALYST COMMUNICATION

» Adam Duran
» www.CatalystCommunicationsGroupInc.com
» 2018 - 2019 Up 44%
» Industry - Commercial Security Systems

### CHANEY CONSTRUCTION

» Jim and Amy Chaney
» www.ChaneyConstructionTX.com
» 2018 - 2019 Up 19%
» Industry - Home Builder

### CITYWIDE MECHANICAL

» Terrance Thomas
» www.CityWide-Mechanical.com
» 2018 - 2019 Up 118%
» Industry - Heating and Air

### CK ELECTRIC
» Chad Kudlacek
» www.CKElectricOmaha.com
» 2018 - 2019 Up 25%
» Industry - Electrician

### COLAW FITNESS
» Charles and Amber Colaw
» www.ColawFitness.com
» 2018 - 2019 Up 15%
» Industry - Fitness Gym

### COMPASS ROOFING
» Robert Alsbrooks & Sonny Ordonez
» www.CompassRoofing.com
» 2018 - 2019 Up 103%
» Industry - Commercial and Residential Roofing

### COMPLETE CARPET
» Nathan & Toni Sevrinus
» www.CompleteCarpetTulsa.com
» 2017 - 2019 Up 298%
» Industry - Carpet Cleaning

### COMFORT PRO
» Steve Bagwell
» www.ComfortPro-Inc.com
» 2018 - 2019 Up 28%
» Industry - Heating and Air

### D&D HOMES - 36%
» Dave Tucker
» https://midsouthhomebuilder.com/

### FULL PACKAGE MEDIA
» 2016 - 2020 - From a Startup with $0 of Annual Revenue to $1,365,000 in Annual Sales
» 2016-2017 - 1,065% Growth Rate
» 2017-2018 - 118% Growth Rate
» 2018-2019- 11% Growth Rate
» 2019-2020 - 38% Growth Rate

### GREEN COUNTRY MEDICAL WASTE - 188%

» Chad Clifton
» GreenCountryMedicalWaste.com

### GEI UTILITY CONSTRUCTION - 112%

» Levi Gable
» GEI-USA.com

### KELLY CONSTRUCTION GROUP - 43%

» Jon Kelly
» KellyConstructionGroup.com

### KRC SQUARED - 156%

» Keith Reicherter
» KRCSquared.com

### LAKE MARTIN MINI MALL:

» 2020 - 2021 - 63%

### PEAK BUSINESS VALUATION - 39.6%

» Ryan & Kelli Hutchins
» 925-787-9608
» https://peakbusinessvaluation.com

### PRIMO - 214%

» Tyler Hallblade
» (480) 378-0800
» primotrailer.com

### REVITALIZE MEDICAL SPA - 42%

» Lindsay Blankenship
» Crista Hobbs
» https://revitalizemedicalspa.com/

### SECURITY GLASS BLOCK - 47%

» Nick and Brianna Behselich
» SecurityGlassBlockWI.com

### SIERRA POOLS:

» $912,014.51
» $1,585,304.42
» 58% growth

**SKY HOUSE CONSTRUCTION - 55%**

» Jeff Pell
» SkyHouseCompany.com

**STUDIO C ARCHITECTURE - 189%**

» Cherri Pitts
» StudioCArch.com
» **THE LEADERSHIP INITIATIVE**
» Back to Basics Builders - 231%
» Joe and Sarah Burbey
» BacktoBasicsBuilders.com

**THE LAWYER JAMES - 73.1%**

» James DeCristofaro
» Thelawyerjames.com

**THERAPEUTIC TOUCH - 116%**

» Annie Leuba
» https://therapeutictouchfacials.com/

**WINDOW NINJAS - 61%**

» Gabe Salinas
» Windowninjas.com

**YELLOWSTONE BASIN CONSTRUCTION - 107%**

» Jake Brosovich
» YBConstruction.com

# APPROVED VENDORS

### 3D RENDERING

» Pools and Outdoor Living - https://www.structurestudios.com/ software/3d-swimming-pool-design-software

» https://www.sketchup.com/

### 3RD PARTY FINANCING

» Home Remodeling - https://www.suntrust.com/loans/home-improvement

» Medical - https://www.carecredit.com/

### ACCOUNTING FIRMS:

» CCK - https://www.cckcpa.com/

» Hood & Associates - https://www.HoodCPAs.com

### BANKING - COMMERCIAL

» First Pryority Bank

» Mikel

» (918) 640-4353

» https://www.firstpryoritybank.com/

» mhoffman@firstpryority.com

### BOOK PUBLISHING:

» Ingram Sparks - https://www.ingramspark.com/

### BUSINESS CARDS:

» MyMetalBusinessCards.com

» Vista Print - www.vistaprint.com

### CHARITIES THAT DON'T SUCK

» St. Jude - https://www.stjude.org/

» March of Dimes - https://www.marchofdimes.org/index.aspx

» Compassion International - www.compassion.com

» Safari Mission - www.safarimission.org

### CLOTHING APPAREL

» Ambition Co. - (918) 638-2804 - http://ambitionco.com/

### CREDIT CARD PROCESSING:

» Tyler - 918-402-6766

» Website Link - https://www.thrivetimeshow.com/credit-card/

**CUSTOMER RELATIONSHIP MANAGEMENT SOFTWARE**

» Software for Contractors - Housecall Pro www.housecallpro.com
 - *ONLY has chat support. No phone number for customer service
» Field Edge - HVAC - Used by Snow Bear Heat and Air - https://
 fieldedge.com/
» Email Invoicing
» Pricing
» Upsell Checklist

**FINANCIAL ADVISORS:**

» Edward Jones - www.edwardjones.com

**FRANCHISING/LICENSING:**

» OXIFresh.com - https://www.thrivetimeshow.com/oxifresh/
» TipTopK9.com - www.TipTopK9.com
» Flow Photos--www.flowphotos.com

**FUNDING FOR BUSINESS OWNERS:**

» Kabbage.com - www.Kabbage.com

**FUNDING FOR CUSTOMERS:**

» https://signup.gethearth.com/

**GPS TRACKING:**

» Verizon - www.verizon.com   - GPS Link
» In Touch - https://intouchgps.com/ - Also helpful for Routing
» Moto Safety - https://www.motosafety.com/

**HOTELS:**

» Casino - https://www.riverspirittulsa.com/hotel/
» Renaissance - https://renaissance-hotels.marriott.com/
» Holiday Inn - Aquarium - https://www.ihg.com/
 holidayinnexpress/hotels/us/en/jenks/tuljs/hoteldetail?cm_
 mmc=GoogleMaps-_-EX-_-US-_-TULJS

**INSURANCE:**

» Life Insurance - New York Life - Jason Dent - 918-408-8017
» Workmans Comp - Gallagher - 918-630-0457
 (Elephant in the Room and OxiFresh)

**JOB POSTS:**

» Indeed: www.indeed.com
» Craigslist: www.craigslist.com

**LEGAL:**

» Winters & King

    Wes Carter - Attorney - 918-494-6868

    Website Link - www.WintersKing.com

**MODELS:**

» Linda Layman - https://www.lindalaymanagency.com/

**OVERHEAD MUSIC:**

» Custom Channels - www.customchannels.net

**PARTY SUPPLIES**

» Party Pro - Tulsa - https://www.partyprorents.com/

**SIGNATURE DIGITAL ASSISTANCE**

» Docusign - https://www.docusign.com/

**STICKERS**

» Sticker Mule - stickermule.com

**SURVEILLANCE**

» ActivTrak - https://activtrak.com

» Nest - https://nest.com/

**WEBSITE TRACKING**

» Lucky Orange - www.LuckyOrange.com

» ActivTrak - https://www.activtrak.com

**PAYROLL:**

» PayChex - www.paychex.com

» PrimePay - primepay.com

**PHONE RECORDING:**

» Clarity Voice

    Heather - 248-436-3435

    Website Link - https://www.thrivetimeshow.com/clarity/

**PODCASTING:**

» Libsyn - http://libsyn.com/

» Podcast Equipment 101

**PRINTING:**

» Vista Print - www.vistaprint.com

» Tulsa Boomerang - https://www.boomerangprinting.net/

» FedEx (Regional) - https://www.fedex.com/global/choose-location.html
» MPix (16x20 pieces) - www.mpix.com
» Post Up Stand - https://www.postupstand.com/
» Sharp Printers - Bud Taha - 918-855-6111
» Flannigan - mybulkmail.com

### PROJECT MANAGEMENT SOFTWARE

» ECI Mark Systems (used by Shaw Homes)- https://www.ecisolutions.com/home-builders-land-developers/marksystems

### RETARGETING ADVERTISEMENTS

» Adroll - Website Link - www.Adroll.com

### SALES LIST

» Sales Genie - www.salesgenie.com

### SHOPPING CART

» Shopify - https://www.shopify.com/

### SOCIAL MEDIA MANAGEMENT

» Hootsuite - http://hootsuite.com/

### TEXTING:

» Twilio - https://www.twilio.com/
» Zipwhip - https://www.zipwhip.com/

### TRANSCRIPTION

» Rev - $1.50 per minute -
» Temi - $.30 per minute -

### T-SHIRTS:

» Custom Ink
» Website Link - www.CustomInk.com

### UNIFORMS

» Amazon Essentials for Uniforms - www.amazon.com
» Cintas - https://www.cintas.com/

### VOICEMAIL:

» Sly Broadcast - https://www.slybroadcast.com/

### WEBSITE HOSTING:

» GoDaddy - https://www.godaddy.com/partners/domain-investors

# EXAMPLE TO-DO LIST

- Call Jonathan - Revolution - Pause his Indeed Advertisements
- Call Jonathan - Thrivetime Show Testimonials - Add this video https://www.youtube.com/watch?v=brRXjUTp15Q&t=1s to this page https://www.thrivetimeshow.com/testimonials/ (replace their previous testimonial)
- Call Will - 24/7 Disaster - About adding 100 articles per month - would like to see disasterherotulsa.com on the keywords list for companies also. Thanks.
- Call the Roads Church - I still have a question about Relentless. although the Relentless page doesn't show up, it still shows under the list of ministries. How do I make it disappear from that list? (I have attached a screenshot of what I am talking about.
- DEEP DIVE - Write questions for Dan Schawbel - Interviewing 12/10
- DEEP DIVE - Write questions for Nick Symmonds - Interviewing 12/12
- DEEP DIVE - Write questions for Brad Lomenick - Interviewing on 12/19
- DEEP DIVE - Write questions for Pastor Larry Osborne - Interviewing on 1/9
- DEEP DIVE - Write questions for Kevin Kelly - Interviewing on 12/18
- DEEP DIVE - Call Wendy - https://docs.google.com/document/d/1savlbPtgfhkFDrpsFROe91zPDxx8Zse3Eis1sSVW4iM/edit?usp=sharing
- Call Vanessa - Charge Tim Redmond for PettisBuilders.com and add to client roster
- Call Vanessa - Verify we are charging Tim Redmond for Electric Techs
- Deep Dive - Thrivetime Show - Write questions for Pastor Randy Frazee
- DEEP DIVE - Thrivetime Show - Write questions for Jon Gordon - https://docs.google.com/document/d/1uvGi7OAwPrP1J6cQJiKZuhYocXFrGLjqoSaCZOibG6Y/edit?usp=sharing - Interviewing 12/18/18
- DEEP DIVE - Thrivetime Show - Write the questions for Andy Bernstein - https://docs.google.com/document/d/151Uo3d3ldxp_qC3SpMDB2XdllmrWT6A_LeX1frEetok/edit?usp=sharing - Interviewing 12/17
- DEEP DIVE - Thrivetime Show - Write the questions for Jeff Bethke - if we can talk about our family teams venture (parenting and family resources) that'd be great - Interviewing 12/13
- DEEP DIVE - Thrivetimeshow - Write questions for Dan Millman (See Brady Boyd questions) - https://docs.google.com/document/d/1BFCa_HtPxPqyx5tn9lRapYBy8qhEs5OBdKcJ_wzolO0/edit?usp=sharing - Interviewing 12/11
- Call Sidney - Confirm Christmas Party details with Sydney 2. Call Marshall to confirm the details for Christmas Party
- Call Vanessa Provide the following documents for One Fire Meeting - https://docs.google.com/document/d/1d-Ng3KUNPpQDJC1R2waJIXAU4aMSG38rcPUGViaSs2E/edit?usp=sharing
- DEEP DIVE - Edit Score Bball Book - https://docs.google.com/document/d/1PyKf5ibBy2DQz_xkASOfLI132KsY6Miri2QzfQMzUYc/edit?usp=sharing
- Record - Intro Rap Songs (Send over to Jonathan)
- Write Noah letter of recommendation - https://docs.google.com/document/d/1LcKny0eVTUfrNUigyu60K0GYMoxvgP9JG4De9lFmOro/edit?usp=sharing
- Call Syndication Services
- DEEP DIVE - Add to Dream 100 1. Relevant Cultural Product People 2. Add Radio Station Syndication Services
- Call Mac - Oklahoma City - Radio Show
- Home - Add songs to office playlist
- Call Wes - Tip Top K9 - Wes - Begin FDD Process 1. Costs? 2. Timeline
- Call Jonathan - Connect with Vanessa about buying a flip house
- Call Jonathan - Books in the Elephant In The Room Stores (1. Signs for Store 2. Books to Stock 3. Initial Order Amount
- DEEP DIVE - Prune the FDD - https://docs.google.com/document/d/1UD_KiXqKpeuM89Aut76lH9JvEt1ZRYAkctz3eBQPcEs/edit?usp=sharing
- Clay - Sam Adams - Get Aaron to have Glenn sign the "Request for Issuance of an Active Provisional Sales Associate"
- Record - Kvell - Edit the audio into commercial - Looking forward to hearing your feedback. https://drive.google.com/drive/folders/17mDxqQfoKiJzjPjK3y4RM9_QsG1QobYH?usp=sharing"
- Call Vanessa - Look into buying an ASCAP license
- DEEP DIVE - Create Elephant In The Room - Shadow Itinerary (Plan for every visit) 2. Screens, etc.
- DEEP DIVE - Thom Clark Stories - https://docs.google.com/document/d/1zIYSHVAqxVVS9RA8IL0HFEqzOAAVRWvA_Fz6juH_Fl9o/edit?usp=sharing
- DEEP DIVE - Yelp Breakdown - https://docs.google.com/document/d/1pwFWEPjV8Api2IakSGjTmE1uy2B_Qdx-rxmTWeccQ-A/edit?usp=sharing
- DEEP DIVE - Elephant In The Room - Create On-Boarding Checklists 2. Discovery Days
- "Record - Kvell - Edit the audio into commercial - Looking forward to hearing your feedback. https://drive.google.com/drive/folders/17mDxqQfoKiJzjPjK3y4RM9_QsG1QobYH?usp=sharing"""
- Record - Edit Morgan Freeman Voice over - https://www.dropbox.com/sh/yir9h5iif0g7n2h/AADIMhyY3sbQcwNg0HQgPSBMa?dl=0
- Record - Morgan Freeman Voice over (edited) https://www.dropbox.com/s/sjxlu4dgnpu9zku/Dr.%20Zoellner%20Named%20Said%20Correctly%20-%20Morgan%20Freeman.mp3?dl=0
- Record - Edit Samuel L Jackson Reads - https://www.dropbox.com/s/oxsssuqs0b3u36f/092418ThrivetimeSchool_SamJackson.wav?dl=0
- Call Jonathan - Answering a Thriver question
- Call Jonathan - Review Rashad Jennings questions - https://docs.google.com/document/d/1TcUFue76YXar8mrqBEWN0FyLyxWTdNVa1tidWgaKOvc/edit?usp=sharing
- Call Jonathan - Ordering TLC business cards
- Call Steve - Move Wednesdays from 11 AM to 3 PM for Sam Adams Realty
- Call Kendal with Clay Staires - Recommendation
- Call Joel Wiland - Interview for podcast - Blaine Bartel
- Call Vanessa - Bathroom Fixes - https://docs.google.com/document/d/1vjjl-oihpwB2QXkPyXAEh19zKo-qbhpuHIN8r7uBOKM/edit?usp=sharing
- Call Debbie - Thrive quarterly review - June 1st at 8am
- Call Vanessa - OneFire - Prepare for meeting - https://docs.google.com/document/d/1SjVcPcEk9aYPOEnd4HtqhcQDEMhLyRJnWtJolHKaVFg/edit?usp=sharing
- Call Tim w FC - https://docs.google.com/spreadsheets/d/1STSFRIxxQ5tStXTNFjPYYsQVTtalbVJdAPrHGsLgebY/edit?usp=sharing
- DEEP DIVE - The Roads - Audit Praise and Worship Service (Bethel) - 1. https://www.youtube.com/watch?v=xCjH8tL87Os&list=PLNpqb6N1H8V2ZNrt7CjaMgH8Bersc-RAx 2. https://www.youtube.com/watch?v=ZTrBnnSbsfk
- Call Jonathan Barnett - Jack Huffman email
- Call Jonathan Barnett - Download - https://www.dropbox.com/sh/78nahnm0fcar0zh/AAAJlIRR3NJszQoCYNgYJQ-Na?dl=0
- DEEP DIVE - Updated Dream 100 Podcasts - https://docs.google.com/spreadsheets/d/1n-t_GsefPkTnrP-1-6EaVCb0Vjc72i656i-3nfpcfZw/edit?usp=sharing
- Fix Aubrey's laptop
- Call Eric Chupp - Top 5 podcasts on iTunes - https://docs.google.com/document/d/1mJOeQtp8GLf-0UrwLpuYTxhKPRKCtxFZGZ_bFDam9l8/edit?usp=sharing
- Call Jonathan - Create OxiFresh Landing Page on ThrivetimeShow (today, much easier - grab images from new.oxifresh.com
- DEEP DIVE - Elephant - Create Discovery Day Path (see Oxi Fresh Itinerary)
- Call Brian Gibson - Hammer of Deal - 80/10/10 - New LLC
- Call Brian Chalkin - Book a time to meet
- Call KPAM - Chris Kelly - Get into other markets (now we are in itunes Top 10)
- Call Wes Carter - Order trademark for Sam Adams Realty
- DEEP DIVE - Podcast Book Landing Page Creation
- Call Wes - Do Your Job - Action Steps

# EXAMPLE CALENDAR

| , Official Clay Clark Calendar | **Thu Oct 3, 2019 (Central Time - Chicago)** |
|---|---|

**4am**
- Clay works out
  4am - 5am

**5am**
- Clay "Meta" Time - CC
  4:45am - 5:30am

**6am**
- Coaches Meeting
  6am - 7am

**7am**
- Clay meets with Clay Staires - CC
  7am - 8am
- Clay meets with Josh Living Water
  7am - 8am

**8am**
- Clay meets with Kat and Adam - Kat Design - CC
  8am - 9am

**9am**
- Clay meets with Trinity i Cory & Amber - CC
  9am - 10am

**10am**
- Clay Meets with Paul Hood
  10am - 11am

**11am**
- Clay meets Pastor Chad Everett
  11am - 12pm

**12pm**
- Brett Denton - Weekly Call - CC
  12pm - 1pm
- SEO Inc & Thrivetime Show Weekly Meeting
  12pm - 1pm

1pm - 2pm

1pm - 2pm Clay meets with Group

2pm - 2:30pm

2:15pm - 3pm

3pm - 4pm Clay meets with Marco Hoab

4pm - 5pm

5pm - 6pm

6pm - 7pm

7pm - 9pm

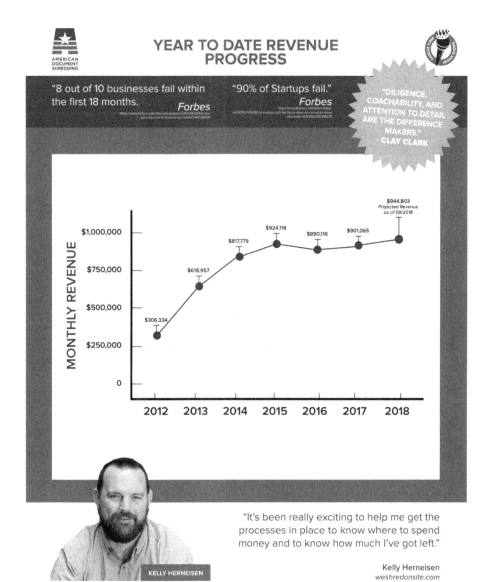

# YEAR TO DATE REVENUE PROGRESS

"8 out of 10 businesses fail within the first 18 months."
*Forbes*

"90% of Startups fail."
*Forbes*

"DILIGENCE, COACHABILITY, AND ATTENTION TO DETAIL ARE THE DIFFERENCE MAKERS."
- CLAY CLARK

MONTHLY REVENUE

$1,000,000 — 
$750,000 — 
$500,000 — 
$250,000 — 
0 — 

$306,334
$618,957
$817,779
$924,118
$890,116
$901,065
$944,803 Projected Revenue as of 09/2018

2012 2013 2014 2015 2016 2017 2018

"It's been really exciting to help me get the processes in place to know where to spend money and to know how much I've got left."

Kelly Herneisen
*weshredonsite.com*

260

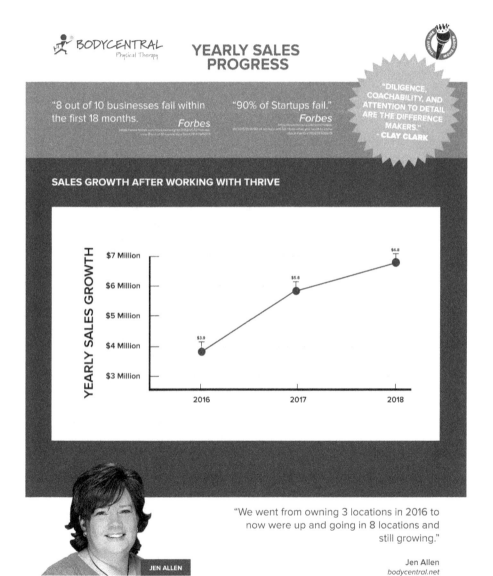

## YEARLY SALES PROGRESS

BODYCENTRAL
Physical Therapy

"8 out of 10 businesses fail within the first 18 months.
*Forbes*

"90% of Startups fail."
*Forbes*

"DILIGENCE, COACHABILITY, AND ATTENTION TO DETAIL ARE THE DIFFERENCE MAKERS."
- CLAY CLARK

### SALES GROWTH AFTER WORKING WITH THRIVE

YEARLY SALES GROWTH

$7 Million
$6 Million
$5 Million
$4 Million
$3 Million

$3.9    2016
$5.8    2017
$6.8    2018

"We went from owning 3 locations in 2016 to now were up and going in 8 locations and still growing."

JEN ALLEN

Jen Allen
*bodycentral.net*

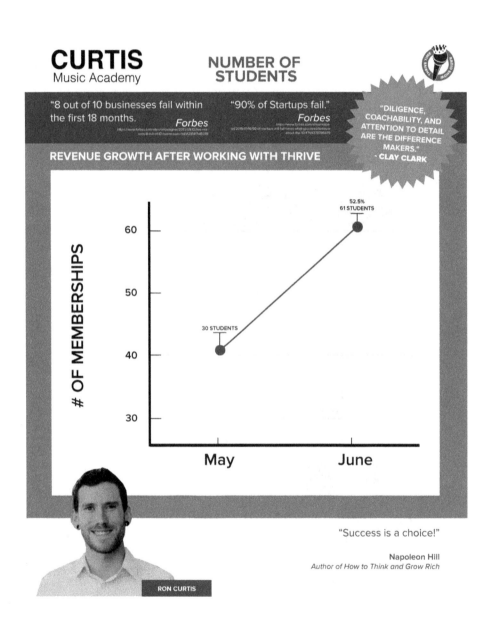

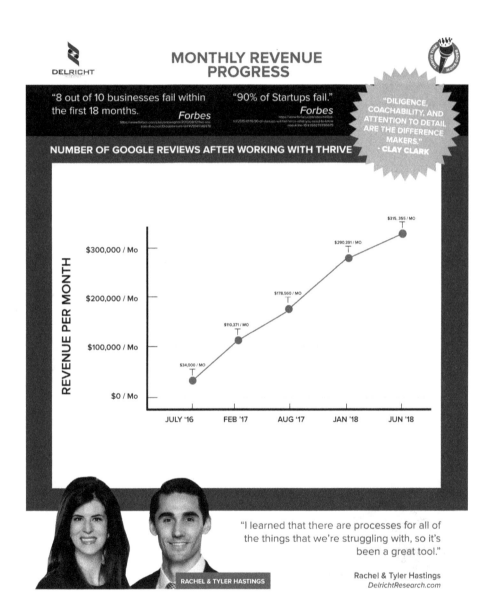

# MONTHLY REVENUE PROGRESS

**DELRICHT**

"8 out of 10 businesses fail within the first 18 months." *Forbes*

"90% of Startups fail." *Forbes*

"DILIGENCE, COACHABILITY, AND ATTENTION TO DETAIL ARE THE DIFFERENCE MAKERS." - CLAY CLARK

## NUMBER OF GOOGLE REVIEWS AFTER WORKING WITH THRIVE

REVENUE PER MONTH

- $34,000 / MO — JULY '16
- $110,371 / MO — FEB '17
- $178,560 / MO — AUG '17
- $290,391 / MO — JAN '18
- $315,355 / MO — JUN '18

"I learned that there are processes for all of the things that we're struggling with, so it's been a great tool."

Rachel & Tyler Hastings
*DelrichtResearch.com*

RACHEL & TYLER HASTINGS

RUSH TO REVENUE
Money Cures All Problems

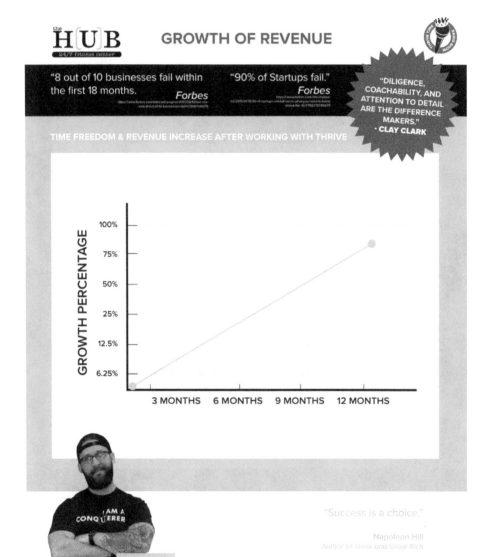

# GROWTH OF REVENUE

**TIME FREEDOM & REVENUE INCREASE AFTER WORKING WITH THRIVE**

"8 out of 10 businesses fail within the first 18 months. *Forbes*

"90% of Startups fail." *Forbes*

"DILIGENCE, COACHABILITY, AND ATTENTION TO DETAIL ARE THE DIFFERENCE MAKERS." - CLAY CLARK

GROWTH PERCENTAGE

100%
75%
50%
25%
12.5%
6.25%

3 MONTHS    6 MONTHS    9 MONTHS    12 MONTHS

"Success is a choice."

Napoleon Hill
Author of Think and Grow Rich

LUKE OWENS

# TIME FREEDOM & REVENUE GROWTH

"8 out of 10 businesses fail within the first 18 months.
*Forbes*

"90% of Startups fail."
*Forbes*

"DILIGENCE, COACHABILITY, AND ATTENTION TO DETAIL ARE THE DIFFERENCE MAKERS."
- CLAY CLARK

## REVENUE & TIME FREEDOM INCREASE AFTER WORKING WITH THRIVE

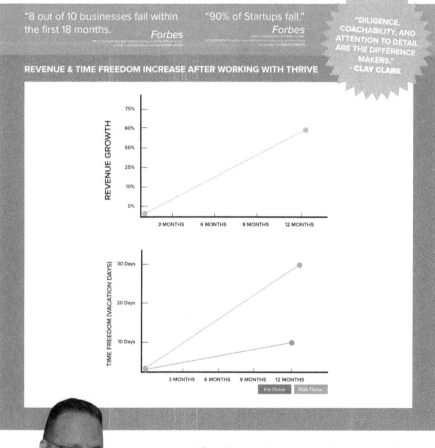

"There's something to learn for everybody."

Kevin Lewis
*LewisRoofing.com*

KEVIN LEWIS

266

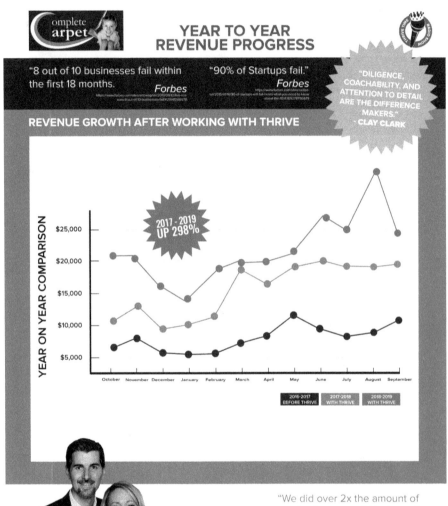

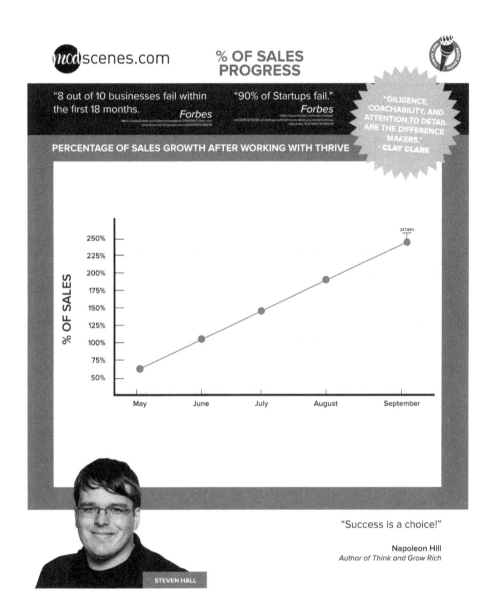

"Success is a choice!"

Napoleon Hill
*Author of Think and Grow Rich*

268

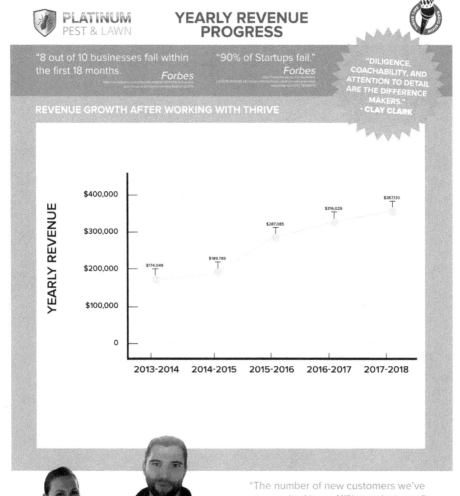

"The number of new customers we've had is up 411% over last year."

Jared & Jennifer Johnson
PlatinumPestandLawn.com

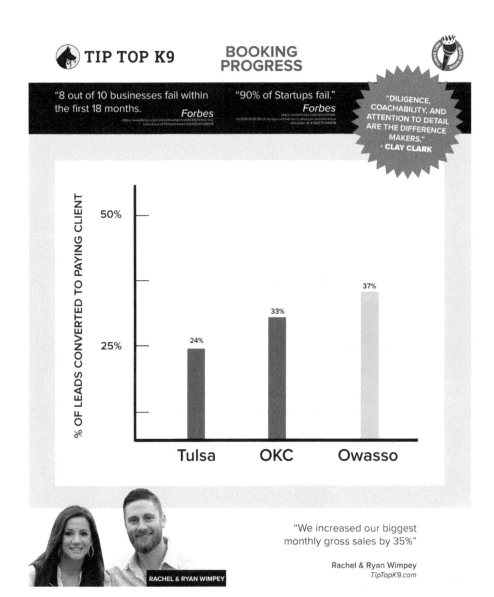

# TIP TOP K9

## BOOKING PROGRESS

"8 out of 10 businesses fail within the first 18 months. *Forbes*

"90% of Startups fail." *Forbes*

"DILIGENCE, COACHABILITY, AND ATTENTION TO DETAIL ARE THE DIFFERENCE MAKERS."
- CLAY CLARK

**% OF LEADS CONVERTED TO PAYING CLIENT**

50%

25%

| Tulsa | OKC | Owasso |
|-------|-----|--------|
| 24%   | 33% | 37%    |

RACHEL & RYAN WIMPEY

"We increased our biggest monthly gross sales by 35%"

Rachel & Ryan Wimpey
*TipTopK9.com*

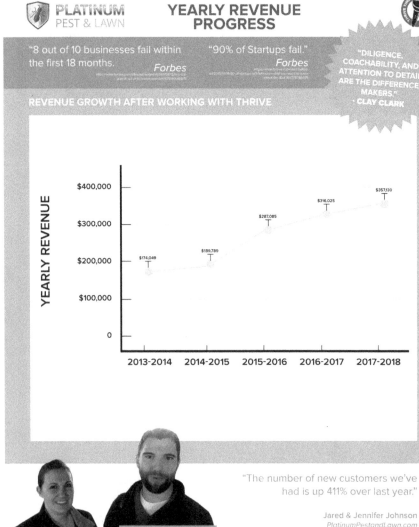

## PLATINUM PEST & LAWN
# YEARLY REVENUE PROGRESS

"8 out of 10 businesses fail within the first 18 months.
*Forbes*

"90% of Startups fail."
*Forbes*

"DILIGENCE, COACHABILITY, AND ATTENTION TO DETAIL ARE THE DIFFERENCE MAKERS."
- CLAY CLARK

**REVENUE GROWTH AFTER WORKING WITH THRIVE**

YEARLY REVENUE

- $400,000
- $300,000
- $200,000
- $100,000
- 0

2013-2014: $174,049
2014-2015: $189,789
2015-2016: $287,085
2016-2017: $316,025
2017-2018: $357,130

JARED & JENNIFER JOHNSON

"The number of new customers we've had is up 411% over last year."

Jared & Jennifer Johnson
*PlatinumPestandLawn.com*

CPSIA information can be obtained
at www.ICGtesting.com
Printed in the USA
FSHW021112040421

9 780998 443522